THE ACCIDENTAL PLUS ONE DOWN UNDER

Travel Tales from a Trailing Spouse Book 2

The Accidental Plus One

ALISON RIPLEY CUBITT

Lambert Nagle Media

DEDICATION
For Sarah and Ben, the Annetts, Hugh, Sandie, Jennifer and Jamie — our
extended family Down Under. And a big shout out to Rona and John, our
support crew.

DISCLAIMER
This book is based on my personal memories and experiences. I've tried
to recount events accurately, but as memory is fallible, some dialogue has
been recreated. To protect the privacy of individuals, names, places, or
dates may have been changed.

Here She Goes (Again)

It's New Year's Eve 2019. Normal people on 31 December would be getting suited and booted for the biggest night of the year. But we (that's me and my other half, known as Bryan Brown (BB) Lookalike, aren't normal people. I'm up at silly o'clock, veering between my weird going away rituals and working through a departure checklist.

I got my one last hike in yesterday, walking across the water meadows and along the muddy path beside the River Itchen, telling the swans I'd see them in the summer. There's no time for an outing this morning, so I clean, empty the fridge as well as scrub my boots, in anticipation at being hauled over by biosecurity in Perth, Western Australia. As we live in the country, I will be ticking "yes" to the "Have you been on a farm.?"— question.

The closer to departure time, the less rational I become. I ignore my packing list and go rogue, stuffing my bag with extra clothes for "just in case". Then I check the security system for the umpteenth time, as well as the timer switches on the lights, even though I know they're all working perfectly. With one hour to go, I flick back to practical me. It's time to shower and get dressed in my long-haul travelling clothes, which have been hanging up in the bathroom since last night. There isn't so much as a sequin on today's outfit and my "going out" shoes are disappointing—built for walking hundreds of extra steps to our departure gate, rather than dancing.

There's some last-minute squeezing of extra toiletries into my big suitcase before assembling my hand luggage with all the electronics and chargers. It's 8.15 and time for what is known as the "Idiot Check" in our house. As well as going room to room to look for stray chargers, I try to figure out what important item I left in a safe place and where that safe place is. Then I turn off all the appliances at the wall, including the emptied fridge. And then I remember my noise-cancelling headphones, hidden in a cupboard in the spare room.

The sitting room and kitchen are cosy and inviting. The only things missing are some appliances, but the two armchairs and sofas that are staying look ready for us to sit down in and relax. Only that's not going to be happening today or for the foreseeable future. It could be as long as five months before I next cross this threshold.

Five months is no big deal, I tell myself. Through the front window I see headlights and a car coming up our driveway. I set sentimental me aside. It's showtime.

'He's here,' I call out.

'On my way,' BB Lookalike says, carrying each suitcase down the stairs and out towards the front door. I take one last look around, before remembering to turn the central heating down, so that it's just warm enough to keep the pipes from freezing. I walk out the front door with my hand luggage, lock up, without so much as a glance at the house and head towards the waiting taxi.

On the one hand it's weird to be in the back of a taxi

on New Year's Eve driving on the M3 to Heathrow airport, but on the other, I'm excited to be escaping England in the depths of winter. There's a steady stream of traffic which builds, the closer we get to the M25, London's orbital ring road, but as there are far fewer vehicles on the road as it's holiday time, we zip through the shortcut from Terminal 5 to Terminal 2 in good time.

We check in for the Qantas non-stop flight to Perth departing at 11.55am and are rolling down the runway on time. The plane is full and there are many families with young children on board. It's a popular flight for parents with infants, as although it's a brutal flight time of 16 hours, at least it's over in one long hop, if your destination is Perth. By the time the New Year's Eve parties in the UK are in full swing, I'm picking my way through dinner. It's only right we see the New Year in with a glass of fizz.

'Here's to another adventure,' I say.

'Melbourne The Sequel,' BB Lookalike says as we clink plastic glasses. (That drunk in the bar in Montreal who mistook him for Australian actor Bryan Brown has a lot to answer for as the name has stuck).

'Take 2,' I say, putting my pretend champagne flute down on my tray table, before bringing my left hand down on my right in the style of a clapperboard.

As the crew removes our meal trays, I turn to BB Lookalike, but his head is slumped to one side and he's fast asleep. I'm envious of his ability to sleep anywhere. I struggle to sleep on planes so I make use of the time to catch up on all the films and TV series I've missed. I pick *Chernobyl*, the five-part docu-drama about the 1986 nuclear disaster. It's hardly a cheery subject, but as I lived through the event, this is a chance to find out what really happened.

I watch open-mouthed at the disturbing revelations. By the time I come up for air, we're over the Indian Ocean.

The extent of the death toll at the reactor site is news to me. Two staff were killed in the explosion and 28 others died within three months of Acute Radiation Sickness. Their protective clothing was primitive and they worked with neither breathing apparatus nor chemical suits. The ill-equipped workers made a personal sacrifice, putting their lives on the line for the greater societal good. If the accident had occurred in the West, where individual rights are valued above any notion of collective responsibility, how many of those workers would have stayed to save the world?

I had no idea how close we came to nuclear anni-hilation.

I'm lucky to be here, I think. I snap back to the present as the lights turn on in the cabin and we are served a hot breakfast. BB Lookalike yawns and stretches,

'Are we nearly there yet?' I pull up the route map on my TV screen.

'Two hours to go,' I say. I spend the rest of the trip watching cookery shows as well as the route map. Once we land and line up at the air bridge at Perth and come to a stop, a laid-back voice on the PA system announces:

'Folks, you'll have noticed we're an hour ahead of schedule. Apologies for the bumps along the way, but thanks to that tailwind, we've just set the record on this route of 15 hours 17 minutes.' As one, we plonk our hand luggage down and burst into spontaneous applause.

The UK and Australia suddenly feel a whole lot closer.

At biosecurity I'm hauled aside to have my walking boots inspected. The officer isn't interested in my horse-riding gear. He scrutinises my boot cleaning efforts, shakes his head and takes the boots away. Five minutes later he comes back with them looking immaculate.

That's one way to get your boots cleaned properly.

By the time we get to the Ramada hotel in Scarborough it's lunchtime on New Year's Day. Reception gives us an early check-in so we hit the shower and head for the beach. I'm desperate for an open-water swim, but there's a stiff gale blowing off the Indian Ocean and too much surf for me. I'm also put off by the alarming signs to "watch out for dugites". I've never heard of them before but discover they're a species of venomous brown snake found along the sand dunes. I knew about the potential hazards in the water but hadn't reckoned on being bitten as I made my way down to the sea. We make do with a walk along the foreshore instead.

After dinner in a restaurant overlooking the ocean, our strategy of choosing New Year's Day rather than New Year's Eve for our first night in Australia, works. All the party animals who had a big night out must need their beauty sleep. The only thing that wakes us up is jetlag. We're up early for our 8.30am four-hour flight. We land at Melbourne in a pall of tangerine-coloured smoke.

2

A Place to Call Home

The summer bushfire season started two months early. In November 2019 footage of the Sydney Harbour Bridge and Opera House engulfed in smoke was syndicated around the world. Alarmed by the images, I kept telling myself that Sydney is 880km from Melbourne. But as my priority was to get everything done on my "upping sticks" to-do list, I had failed to grasp the gravity of the devastation in New South Wales and Victoria. And we were in the air when an out-of-control bushfire at Mallacoota, a beach town to the northeast of Melbourne, forced its residents to flee the fire front and head to the beach.

The Australian Defence Force and Victoria Police co-ordinated an emergency rescue plan, landing Black Hawk helicopters next to the boat ramp, airlifting over 400 stranded residents and holidaymakers to an Australian Navy ship, where they were evacuated to safety.

It is only on our first evening in Melbourne, after we've settled into our serviced apartment and had time to sit down and watch the news, that we understand the scale of the destruction. Fifty fires are burning in Victoria, a state the size of the United Kingdom, and five regions, including the Victorian High Country, have been declared disaster areas. The fires are raging east of us in Gippsland and north on the Victorian and New South Wales coasts. Weather forecasters predict extreme fire conditions for this weekend. We're not planning to leave the city but our main concern is air quality.

I go online to research face masks that filter pollutants, as we have to go into town on Friday. Bunnings, a DIY chain, stocks N95 masks, but there's been a run on them and they've sold out. A crimson sun sinks over the horizon and the sky is pink, a beautiful but sombre reminder that we are surrounded by fires raging across the state.

The next day we catch a tram to the city. As we get off the tram and step on to the road, I smell burnt wood and the smoke haze sears my throat. Neither of us have respiratory health conditions, but even so, I'm uneasy, especially as the agency that monitors air quality has warned people to avoid being outside in the city centre.

As soon as we are done, we catch the tram back to St Kilda. We head straight for the shoreline and walk along the boardwalk. The vast expanse of Port Phillip Bay stretches before us and at last we can inhale clean air.

As we walk south towards Elwood, it hits me that it's ten years since the Black Saturday bushfires, which killed 173 people. It was this tragedy that made me homesick for England the first time we lived in Melbourne and became the catalyst for us selling and moving back home. I'm more resilient now than I was back then, but even so, I'm dreading the rest of fire season.

We return via the supermarket to our serviced apartment. I booked this place because it is the cheapest available that comes with a full kitchen. The reviews are good, but what I failed to do was check the location—smack in the middle of one of the busiest road junctions in Melbourne. The air is toxic from the bushfire smoke mixed with diesel and petrol fumes. We keep all the windows shut and run the air-conditioner. At least our bedroom faces away from the street and the venerable air-conditioner blocks out most of the road noise at night, but it doesn't mask the late-night door slamming by fellow guests.

Living in uncomfortable temporary digs is an incentive to find somewhere more permanent to live. We can't wait to get settled, but first we must decide whether to buy or rent. We speak to a mortgage consultant on a conference call.

'How are you going to fund the deposit?' the broker asks.

'With the money we have in super,' I tell him. 'And we'll pay the mortgage with our income, then sell the apartment when we return to the UK.'

The broker says nothing.

What's wrong with that? I think.

'What are you going to live on when you retire?'

'The remainder of the super and the capital from the sale,' we say.

'Look,' he says, 'the length of the average mortgage in Australia is 30 years.'

What he's trying to say is that in 30 years' time you two will be six feet under or in a care home, I think.

'And the banks will worry that neither of you will have enough time left in your working lives to pay the loan back.'

So I was right. But oh, the irony. When I was a humble produc-tion assistant in my twenties, banks couldn't wait to lend me money. Now I'm old and debt free, they don't want to know.

'You need to hang on to an apartment for at least seven years to see any return on your investment,' he tells us.

'And if the market drops when you want to sell, you could lose money. If you had a deposit, that might help.'

It's not the first time we've come up against ageism. We got the same answer from the immigration consultant when we asked if we could reinstate our Permanent Residence, which we lost as we were out of Australia for too long. Silly us, we thought the word "permanent" meant forever, but it turns out it came with a caveat. The immigration adviser was more tactful than the mortgage guy, stressing we'd have to provide proof we could afford private medical insurance once we retired.

We decide we can't be arsed to jump through all the bureaucratic hoops to get Permanent Residence. We already have New Zealand citizenship, which is why we can live, work and apply for Medicare in Australia.

We revert to Plan B, which is to rent. Even though it was my job to find homes for expats when we last lived here, neighbourhoods will have changed in the past eight years. I have a shortlist of areas where we'd like to live but no car to get from A to B. Our intention is to live somewhere with good public transport as we can't afford another car, in addition to the one we left behind in the UK.

We could do with some help. I contact the relocation firm I worked for to book a consultant to line up some properties for rent.

The Hunt Begins

Sarah, our Consultant, plans our viewings to start closest to the city at Port Melbourne, then we'll work our way back to St Kilda, which is 10km from BB Lookalike's work. Twenty km per day is at the limit of his cycling commute.

When it's too wet or cold for the bike, he plans to take a tram.

Being close to the city comes at a price and we expect that our rent will be higher than if we lived in the suburbs. As well as the deposit, as most rental properties come without appliances and furniture, I estimate our setting-up costs, including the rental bond, will be at least $15,000.

We can't wait to move. Life in the serviced apartment is fraught with tension. On Friday night, I hear a young girl sobbing on the step outside our apartment. I sit with her until she is ready to talk. Her family has travelled to Melbourne from country Victoria for a significant event and at the last minute, her special-needs older sister tried to sabotage it. She created such a scene that social services intervened. This girl is having trouble coping, as her older sister's behaviour is too much to bear.

'Is there anyone else in your family you can talk to?' I ask.

'Mum and Dad are dealing with this shit all the time,' she says.

'Do you have maybe an aunty?'

She thinks for a moment. 'Yeah, I have my nana.'

'Nana's are great, aren't they?' I say. She nods. Gradually her tears subside. She looks at me and gives me a watery smile.

'Thanks,' she says.

Poor kid. When one child in a family has special needs and demands their parents' attention, it must be so difficult for their siblings not to feel overlooked.

Sarah picks us up at 9am sharp on Saturday. At the first Open Home viewing, six other couples are waiting, all urgently needing to find somewhere to live. January is the most competitive month to find a rental property as it's when most employees (including BB Lookalike) start their new jobs.

Our only advantage is that we have a relocation agent working on our behalf, who not only knows all the real estate agents, but can vouch for the reference checks and our ability to afford the rent. But in a landlords' market like this one, there will be people prepared to pay over the odds or six months' rent in advance.

One apartment has a transparent all-glass bathroom, including the wall between it and the bedroom.

'To bring more light into the room,' says the Real Estate Agent. 'It's a new trend in hotel design.' Sarah's face is a picture. I'm trying hard not to corpse.

Who wants to see someone take a pee? Or worse? Obviously, these millennials do, as they're glued to their phones, thumbs flying furiously, putting through their online applications. Nor does the Agent's warning that the building has a few "issues" (or defects) put them off. The swimming pool is out of bounds until the ominous-sounding cracks are investigated and fixed. I don't even have to ask BB Lookalike what he thinks of the place as we're both still trying not to laugh.

'I wasn't expecting that,' I say to Sarah and BB Lookalike as we move on to our next viewing, a three-bedroom townhouse on a main road. And it's not just any main road but the Westgate Freeway, which takes heavy goods vehicles to and from the *Spirit of Tasmania* ferry. As the ferry arrives and departs in the early morning or late at night, noisy trucks with airbrakes are a deal-breaker.

'They're moving the terminal to Geelong in 2022,' the Agent says. 'And the house is double-glazed.'

She must be desperate if she believes we'll put up with that racket for two years.

Our final booked viewing is a two-bedroom apartment

inside a listed former sugar mill, which we walk to. Since I was last here, fast-food outlets have multiplied and many of the quirky shops have disappeared. But at least the independent bookshop is still there.

The apartment has a weird layout over two floors, including a mezzanine and is not made any more appealing by beige carpet and bland décor. Sensing that we are going to pass on this one, the Real Estate Agent pipes up:

'I've got another one. It's in St Kilda, with two bedrooms and a study. It's on the top floor of a 1960s block and has amazing views. It's $750 a week, the same price as this property. But there's no gym, pool or yoga studio.' All I hear is the word "study". All BB Lookalike hears is "amazing views". Neither of us could give a hoot about the lack of fancy facilities.

'This is sounding good. When can we see it?'

'I can show you now.'

I try not to get too excited.

'We're going in that direction, anyway,' Sarah says.

We park outside the ten-storey block and glance up. The building, named Questa Heights, is on the Esplanade, two streets back from St Kilda beach. And the apartment we're about to view is on the top floor. So, a penthouse, then. But I curtail my enthusiasm for a moment as there's no denying that the building is in dire need of a paint job and, to my eyes, is ugly, made uglier by a collection of rooftop antennae. An enthusiastic sales agent would describe this place as a "modernist landmark" and a "St Kilda icon", but I'm a philistine when it comes to modernist architecture, especially when it's been neglected, as this block clearly has.

'Once you're inside the apartment you won't even notice what the outside looks like,' Sarah points out.

In the communal area there's peeling paint on the sills and frames of the glass front door, which isn't even locked. It opens onto a grey tiled floor next to the mailboxes. Then there's a second door giving access to the lift and stairs, which I'm relieved to see does require a key. After the lift has creaked its way up, it lands at least an inch below the ninth floor.

That will annoy the movers, I think as I exit the lift and follow the hall around a corner. The Agent must have got there first as the door to the apartment is wide open. We walk into a spacious open-plan room, with the sitting area to the left, the dining area next to it and a kitchen twice the size of the one we have back home. My jaw drops as I take in the 260 degree views. The vast expanse of the blue waters of Port Philip Bay to the front, Port Melbourne to the side, as well as the skyscrapers of the CBD.

We reluctantly drag ourselves away to look at the rest of the apartment. From the office, you can see out to Albert Park. And the two bedrooms at the back look out over the Eastern suburbs and the Dandenong Ranges.

Focus, I tell myself. I try hard to be objective and see what else this place has to offer. I note the two bathrooms, one with a bath, the other with a walk-in shower. The bonus isn't just a shelved study, but a storeroom on the landing for our exclusive use. I don't reckon we'll get a lot of use out of the two balconies, as they'd only just seat two chairs. The Agent has to ask for help to open the door to the front one because of the strength of the wind. We take it in turns to stand on it, as a fierce southerly gale nearly knocks us off our feet. The one at the back is a bit more sheltered. I imagine a cheerful array of plants in this space.

As the Agent mentioned, the rent is $750 a week, our upper price limit, but as this is the average price of all the apartments we've viewed, here we are getting far more bang for our buck. We put our application in on the spot.

When we get back to the serviced apartment, I do some research on what I hope will be our new home. The block was built in 1963 and the architect who designed it built Edgewater Towers, another mid-century landmark in St Kilda. Both buildings are admired by mid-century enthusiasts as well as architects and architectural historians.

Would they be as enthusiastic if they had to live in them? I wonder.

We set our moving date for the third week in January. The apartment comes with a dishwasher, oven and hob. We need to buy a washing machine, dryer, fridge-freezer and beds and that's just the start. The money I had set aside is eaten up in a flash and I blow the budget by $2,000. I console myself that at the end of the five years we're due to be here, we can resell the items.

When we moved to Melbourne from New Zealand in 2005, we took a 40 foot container, all paid for by an employer. Fifteen years on and shipping costs have skyrocketed. This time around it's just us and we are limited to the essential tools of BB Lookalike's work— enough books to fill two offices, as well as kitchen equipment and clothing. As we still have Sarah for another half day and we need some essentials to tide us over until our stuff arrives, she picks me up in her 4WD and we hit up IKEA.

'You can pass everything on when the container arrives,' she says.

If only I was like that, I think. Inevitably, we end up with duplicates. I only give away our third knife sharpener in year five. Despite us buying the cheapest bits of kitchen equipment, only the expandable sieve breaks. And that's only because I treat it like a colander and drain too many potatoes in it, but broken or not, I refuse to replace it and still use it up until the day we move out.

Although I only buy cheap cooking equipment, it's a false economy to do the same with home appliances. All our electronics come from the biggest electrical retailer in the country who offer us a big discount for a bulk order as well as free delivery, which is too good to resist.

BB Lookalike's office desk and chair come from a shop in Richmond specialising in 20th century designer reproductions. We get them for a knock-down price as they are ex-display. The desk weighs a ton, and the delivery guys will struggle to get it into the lift. For the little items I've forgotten, I top up at the many charity shops in the area.

There is a large transient population of temporary residents on work visas as well as restaurants that go out of business offloading crockery and glassware, so I end up with some real finds. We're also fortunate enough to inherit a few pieces from ex-pat friends including a gorgeous wool rug that adds much needed pizzazz to the living room.

When our Real Estate Agent told us she had problems letting the apartment, it didn't surprise me. Not only does the building lack the facilities that many younger renters want, I suspect that the dated décor would have put them off. The kitchen-diner has a 70/80s vibe, with engineered stone black benchtops and a breakfast bar. Over the breakfast bar are two lights with mauve glass lampshades. The cabinetry, which includes a handy pantry, is in a mid-brown veneer, some of which is sun-damaged and showing its age. But I'm still in awe of the kitchen's size, and as we both love to cook, it's perfect for our needs.

Next to the front door is a large hallway cupboard, fitted out as a coat rack and for shoe storage. We appreciate all the storage, even if it looks drab, as modern apartments have next to none.

On the dot of 9am on Saturday 25 January, I'm at reception at the Real Estate Agent's office in Caulfield. I beam at the Agent at the front desk.

'I'm here to collect the keys for 9A/21 The Esplanade,' I say, pronouncing it as "Esplanaid".

'No,' the young Agent says, shaking her head. 'It's pronounced "Esplanard".' She sounds out every syllable, as if dealing with a particularly thick five-year-old.

You don't pronounce lemonade as "lemonard, do you? I don't say to her, as she has the keys I so desperately want. I smile through gritted teeth at her.

'Sign here,' she points. 'And here and here.' I obey her orders, collect the paperwork and the remote control for the carpark, and skip out of there to a waiting Uber. When I arrive back, BB Lookalike is outside the building talking to the delivery drivers from the electrical retailer who have got there early. We've managed to co-ordinate it so that we have a bed, sofas, table and chairs, kitchen equipment, a TV and BB Lookalike's desk and chair delivered on moving day.

I have an ulterior motive to make it look like the apartment has been lived in for a while. We have friends from New Zealand visiting, and if we'd told them it was moving day, they might not have come. It's wonderful to welcome our first guests. We have a celebratory house-warming drink before heading out to eat dinner at Cicciolina's, a St Kilda institution.

This last week of January is a scorcher, with Friday predicted to hit 43C. My happy place temperature-wise is the low 20s as I've had enough sun exposure to last a lifetime and when I go walking, I'm covered up from head to toe. On the Thursday, I go out early in the relative cool, then retreat to the apartment, drawing the blinds to block out the sun and with the air-conditioner on.

The high temperatures are taking their toll on the fires still raging across the state. I catch up with the news that evening. An area bigger than the entire US state of Florida is either burnt or still burning across all Australian states and territories. The scale exceeds my comprehension. And the human cost stretches far beyond our shores when a waterbombing aircraft, flown by a volunteer US crew, crashes, killing all three firefighters.

It's just my luck that on the hottest day of the year I have an appointment at lunchtime at the Department of Social Services in Prahran to apply for our Medicare cards. I need to take a tram and then walk. I set off in hat, sunglasses and long-sleeves and remember to take my water bottle. The walk to the tram stop, 250 metres away, is punishing enough in this heat. Then at the other end I will have a 750-metre walk along Commercial Road.

When the tram drops me off, I immediately regret that I didn't stay on for another couple of stops, as a walk that should have taken me ten minutes takes twenty. As I enter the office building, a wall of cool air hits me. I'm wobbly on my feet. I steady myself. The last thing I want to do is pass out.

Normal body temperature is 37C and I've just walked in 43C. I gulp down half the contents of my water bottle. And then I remember I have to do the same journey in reverse. I wait 45 minutes for my appointment, but I don't care as it's cool in the office.

Afterwards, I check for the nearest tram stop and there's one directly opposite. It's in the full sun and when the tram turns up, it's an old-fashioned one, without air-conditioning.

I'd better toughen up. We've got three more months of this.

White Knuckle Ride

We're walking past a cleared building site three doors down and notice the solid perimeter fence, with a huge advertising hoarding showing an artist's impression of a major development, about to start construction. On the site of what was once the St Moritz ice rink and latterly a hotel, is a project to build two luxury tower blocks of 90 apartments at a cost of $580 million. The project got green lit in 2019 and it's not due for completion until the end of 2022.

So, this is why our agent couldn't let our penthouse apartment, I think. We'll have three years of construction noise to look forward to, but at least it will be quiet at night.

BB Lookalike is due to start teaching in March 2020. In the meantime, we re-connect with old friends as well as family. I'm working from home and discover my local community through my daily walks. I alternate between the beach boardwalk to Elwood, and through the Botanical Gardens as far as Elsternwick, returning via Ripponlea and St Kilda East, which I call the Four Great Bakeries Walk.

It's Sunday and the forecast is for a sunny 21C. As today is BB Lookalike's last chance for a day off before teaching starts at the University of Melbourne, we take a trip down Memory Lane to Williamstown, where we lived between 2006 and 2011. There's a little ferry that leaves from our local pier and as it's a calm day, it'll be fun to take that for once, rather than the tram and train.

There are eight passengers, including us, and two crew. It's the smallest boat I've ever been on that takes paying passengers. The little craft heads out towards Geelong, crossing the shipping lane and turning right towards Williamstown.

You don't grasp the size of Port Phillip Bay until you see it from the back of a small boat. A seven-storey-high container ship, piled with multi-coloured boxes, glides past us. If we got in its way it would swallow us up in seconds. Half an hour later we're pulling up at Gem Pier, next to a forbidding-looking grey ex-warship, HMS *Castlemaine*, repurposed as a museum.

As we walk along the boardwalk, I eye up another little boat to my left, bobbing up and down on the water. I'm glad to see that Gem Pier Seafood, where we bought our fresh fish every Sunday when we lived here, is still going strong. It's too early for lunch so we head off for a walk to work up an appetite.

We turn left out of Gem Pier and walk past the Time-ball Tower on Battery Road. Originally a lighthouse constructed of bluestone, which in 1849 was quarried and cut by convict labour, the tower is grey, rather than blue. The building is grim and austere, in contrast to this shiny, carefree day.

Our route takes us down along the foreshore as far as the Williamstown Botanical Gardens, one of my favourite places in the area. Opened to the public in 1860, the gardens contain rare trees, an ornamental lake and a palm walk. I imagine Victorian-era women walking around the garden in their long dresses, parasols held aloft.

I snap back to the present as we make our way back to Gem Pier where we join the line for a picnic lunch of lobster rolls and Pacific oysters.

This is the life. It feels like we're on holiday.

And that was why living here was lovely, but it felt cut off, as all the buzz happens on the city side of the Westgate Bridge.

We catch the return ferry at 2pm. The temperature has plummeted by ten degrees, the wind has swung around to the south and we head straight into it. Even though we are in the sheltered waters of the bay, the boat is beaten back by the force of the waves as we crash head-on into them. When we turn side-on, the boat pitches then rolls.

If it's this rough in the bay, what must it be like out in open sea? I wonder. I don't know if I can hang on to my lunch.

I wish we'd taken the train back.

As the young captain controls the ferry, looking straight ahead, he pulls out a packet of sandwiches and starts to munch on them, steering with only one hand on the wheel. He's concentrating so hard on the direction of travel, he has no idea about the drama unfolding beside us.

We're sitting at the back in the open air, where I take deep breaths to stave off seasickness as the craft ploughs up to the crest of the waves and plummets down again. As we pass Middle Park on our left, an out-of-control yacht comes shooting out from the shore, barrelling towards us. I lock eyes with the skipper, as he makes a last-ditch attempt to steer his yacht away from our ferry.

'He's going to hit us,' the woman next to me says. We both go to grab a handrail, bracing for impact. At the speed he's going, he'll slice our boat in two and not one person is wearing a lifejacket. As I weigh up whether we'll even survive the impact, the yacht passes behind us with inches to spare. We've been saved, not by any miracle, but by physics. Even though a collision looked inevitable, our boat's engine propelled us forward and out of danger. Those of us still hanging on for dear life at the back of the boat shake our heads in disbelief.

'That was close,' my new friend says.

'I'm going the boring way next time,' I say. Meanwhile at the wheel, the captain is still munching his sandwiches and oblivious to what went on behind and to the side of him.

Once we moor up at St Kilda, I'm first off, vowing to never again set foot on that ferry.

A few days later, BB Lookalike and I are invited to dinner at the home of a former colleague of his, who mentions the recent news out of China. A new virus has been detected, she says, and it is likely we could be impacted by it, here in Australia. Being an optimist, I suggest that it will probably end up being like the SARS (severe acute respiratory syndrome) outbreak in Hong Kong, scary for those affected, but safely contained in South East Asia.

'Life will go on as normal here, I'm sure,' I say. I have never been so wrong.

3

House Arrest

After my Pollyanna remark at the dinner party, I go online. Over 8,000 people caught SARS between 2002 and 2004 with 774 dying, so it was far more serious than I made out. Whatever the impact of this new virus will be, I should have been paying more attention to the news.

The first case of coronavirus in Australia occurred in a man from Wuhan who flew in from Guangzhou in China in late January. In mid-February, Singapore Airlines announced they would be cancelling all flights departing from major Australian cities, including Melbourne, because of the coronavirus outbreak.

It's just one airline. Surely Qantas will keep its connection to the outside world open?

I am about to book my flight back to the UK for the British summer, to get stuff done on the house. I hold off for now.

By 3 March, we are living in crazy times. Supermarket shelves are stripped of essential items like hand sanitiser and toilet paper as would-be preppers stockpile for a future catastrophe. The hashtag #toiletpaper has been trending on Twitter. And Woolworths, our nearest supermarket, is restricting the sale of this item to four packs per customer.

Meanwhile, we make the most of living in a big city, dining out with friends in town and up at Carlton, after a talk from Irish journalist Fintan O'Toole. No mention is made of the new virus, but I'm very aware that sitting in a packed lecture theatre, any one of us could be passing it on to the person sitting next to us.

The following evening, we get together with friends from overseas, who are passing through Melbourne. They seem sanguine about what impact Coronavirus will have on their travels.

The same day, the WHO (World Health Organisation) declares Covid-19 a global pandemic.

The Road to Lockdown

At 7am on Friday 13 March, I'm walking along the Bay Trail, connecting St Kilda and Elwood beaches, listening to the whine of cars roaring around the Melbourne Grand Prix track at Albert Park. Even though I have no interest in motor racing, the Grand Prix is a big deal.

At 7.30am the whine stops.

That's weird.

When I get back from my walk, I check Twitter. Two Formula 1 drivers, Sebastian Vettel and Kimi Räikkönen, have already flown home. On top of that, two McLaren team members have tested positive to Covid-19. At 9am the Victorian State Premier, Daniel Andrews, announces to the media that the event can only be run without spectators.

He's making it up as he goes along. They can't run a race without two of the drivers.

But nobody has yet told the fans gathering outside the main entrance to the park, waving their tickets for practice day. They're blocked from the grounds, but no one will explain why. It takes until 10.30am for the organisers to announce that the event is officially cancelled. They promise ticket holders a full refund, but the fans who've travelled from far and wide will still have to pay for their transport and accommodation.

On 15 March, the day when we would have expected to hear all the hoopla of race day, it's business as usual at a local eatery where we go for a Sunday afternoon cheese-board and wine flight. First thing Monday morning, a live broadcast press conference announces that a State of Emergency now exists in Victoria. And at the same press conference, the Federal government issues an order that all mass gatherings of 500 and over are to be cancelled.

We have no desire to go anywhere with hordes of other people, but the virus hasn't put holidaymakers on cruises off yet, even though passengers who have come back from an overseas port have to self-isolate for 14 days, as do all travellers entering Australia.

Who is going to check up on these people to make sure they're doing the right thing? I wonder.

By the end of the week, the flawed policy for cruise ships comes to a head when just under 3000 holidaymakers are allowed to disembark in Melbourne after a ten-hour delay. The crew on one vessel aren't so lucky as they must stay with their empty ship, which remains anchored in Port Phillip Bay for weeks. We watch it from our front window.

How must the poor crew be feeling, stranded for so long? I ask myself.

In New South Wales, another cruise ship, *Ruby Princess*,

docks in Sydney Harbour and all 2,700 passengers are allowed to leave, catch public transport and international flights. After complaining of feeling unwell, 130 of them test positive for Covid-19. This becomes the biggest single source of infections in the country. As a result of the *Ruby Princess* debacle, the NSW Health Minister, Brad Hazzard, becomes known on social media as "Health Hazzard".

On 20 March 2020, from 9pm, only Australian citizens, Permanent Residents and their immediate families will be permitted to enter the country. I let this sink in.

Even if I could find a flight out, they might not let me back in. The borders are effectively sealed.

Two days later the Victorian Premier makes another announcement that all non-essential services, including clothing retailers, will close on Tuesday evening. I resist the urge to run into the city, as everyone else who watched that press conference will be doing last-minute shopping. I wait until Monday morning, when anyone left working in the city will be inside their offices.

As the tram makes its way along Bourke Street, I notice passers-by scurrying along beside us, heads bowed, staring at the pavement. I'm outside Bourke Street Mall a few minutes before 10am, waiting for the doors to open.

I hit Myer, H&M and David Jones, grabbing gym gear, warm jumpers, thermals and random items of clothing I might need for the next few months, in case this lockdown is going to drag on. There are far fewer shoppers than I expected, so I'm done in less than an hour. It seems crazy to be buying winter clothes when it's still warm enough to swim in the sea, but Melbourne's Four Seasons in One Day reputation can see the temperature veer from the high 30s down to 12C in less than 24 hours.

When I get home, I skim read through what lockdown will mean for us while BB Lookalike runs planning meetings about the feasibility of delivering online courses should universities close. From Monday 30 March, three weeks into the semester, the University of Melbourne switches to online teaching for most of its degree subjects. BB Lookalike, who has come all this way to Australia to teach in person, spends hours modifying his courses. As in-person screenings are an important part of film degrees, he has to make last-minute changes and find films that can be streamed over the internet.

The home office, where BB Lookalike can shut the door, record his lectures and host tutorials, becomes a godsend. I can't imagine what life would be like if our only workspace was the dining room table. Posts on social media discuss tensions at home where one partner works from the bedroom, the other in the kitchen, while both try to keep children occupied. The Victorian government brings the school holidays forward by a week so that families are all at home together. But when remote school starts, it will be a major headache for staff, who must give up their holidays to prepare online courses, and for the students who will have to co-ordinate access to laptops and computers.

One of the non-essential services that's closing will affect yours truly: in-person gyms. With neither kids nor a dog, group exercise classes at the gym are one of my few opportunities to socialise. Now that's been taken away from me, I worry that I will become not only unfit, but socially isolated.

But my gym is one step ahead of me and contacts its members, asking us if we want to borrow exercise equipment as their personal trainers are planning to teach virtual classes. I jump at the chance and enlist BB Lookalike between meetings to help me lug back assorted weights (including two 5kg ones), a bar and a body pump bench.

We stuff the kit into a shopping trolley and between the two of us, manage to drag it all home.

While they won't fix my social isolation, at least virtual classes will mean I can stay fit.

Lockdown 1 31 March to 12 May 2020

As lockdown in Victoria coincides with lockdown in the UK, I hear that one of my gym instructors back in Hampshire has moved all her classes online and is offering them for just £3 each. It's an incredibly generous offer to prioritise our mental well-being ahead of earning extra income from this initiative. I jump at the chance to join in, even though the live classes are at odd times of the day and night for me. It's about the social contact as much as the exercise as I'm doing it with people I know (and some I don't).

I love the way each of us has managed to find somewhere to workout at home, whether that's a kitchen, or a corner of a bedroom. I admire my instructor's immaculate kitchen from afar and enjoy watching her attention-seeking cat staring into the camera. The cat has competition from a pet star of another online exercise class, a demanding dachshund, who plonks himself down theatrically in his basket in the middle of a lesson, then five minutes later gets bored and wants to be let outside.

Unlike the virtual classes from my Melbourne gym, the two classes in Hampshire start with a brief hello. Some of the participants are already friends, whereas others I'm getting to know, but we're all in this together, trying to keep our spirits up and establish order and routine in a world turned upside down by the pandemic. I feel connected to the world I left behind and far less isolated in an Australia that has pulled up the drawbridge.

Lockdown requires all Victorians not working in essential services to work from home. But BB Lookalike and I are already doing that, so the directive just becomes part of our daily rituals.

I wish working from home had been a thing when I was in TV. Work back then was all about presenteeism. Being seen to be working was as important as doing the job.

The other restriction imposed upon us is that we are only permitted one hour of exercise within a 5km radius. This presents us with an immediate problem. We can comply with the rule when we face south, east and north, but become unstuck when looking west, out over Port Phillip Bay.

Are we allowed to go kayaking in the bay if we don't travel further than 5km? I wonder. When we're on the Bay Trail midweek, it seems that we aren't the only ones out and about. I've never seen so many walkers, joggers and cyclists. Surely rowing on the bay will be more isolated, if only I was any good at kayaking.

As well as the hour for exercise, we're allowed to spend another hour shopping for food and essentials. Since the debacle of toilet roll rationing, thanks to the hoarders with their siege mentality, I've become increasingly fed up with supermarkets. They're places to get in and out of as fast as possible. We go masked up and keep our 1.5 metre distance from other shoppers. But when there are too many people in an aisle, we all do a frantic dance, flattening ourselves against the shelves, trying not to breathe when someone wants to get past.

We interpret the rules to suit us, combining exercise and shopping into one two-hour slot. One person per household is allowed to go into a shop or a supermarket, but the rules take no account of those of us without cars, who can't carry all our shopping home without help. BB Lookalike and I get the map out and see that Prahran Market is just within the 5k limit. To get around the rules about two people from the same household shopping together, we split up. One of us buys the deli items and fresh pasta, the other heads off to the vegetable and bread stalls. We team tag the fish and meat sections. To cheer ourselves up, we swap between the various cake stalls, one week buying Italian cannoli, the next, Portuguese custard tarts or chocolate fondants. I'd shop daily at the market if I lived closer. Passing the time of day with the stallholders and talking recipes brings us joy in our increasingly topsy-turvy world, but the best we can manage is a weekly trip.

When Prahran Market releases a statement alerting customers that an infected shopper spent an hour and half at the venue, from 9.40am to 11.15am, coinciding with when we were last there, we heed the advice to get tested, isolate and wait anxiously for our results. I don't even want to think about what it would mean if we tested positive. Meanwhile, the market shuts and is deep cleaned. Thousands of dollars' worth of fresh food must be thrown away and all the staff who were working that day are ordered to isolate for 14 days. The market is mainly made up of small family-run businesses who lose two weeks' income as well as their stock. When we get our negative results, we celebrate by returning to the market as soon as the traders are allowed back.

I make up for a lack of a social life by spending far too much time on social media, especially Twitter. Then there's the distraction of the endless cycle of press conferences on TV, with both the State and Federal governments. The daily local press conferences are sparring matches between the Labour Premier of Victoria and the right-wing news media who regard Daniel Andrews as a communist despot. He thrives on the attacks and bats every question back.

I give up trying to make sense of all the restrictions around Covid-19 and cheer myself up that the hospitality industry is given a lifeline by being permitted to offer take-aways while the pubs and restaurants are closed. It's sad that wait-staff will lose their jobs, but at least kitchen staff can pay their rent. And for diners who don't fancy cooking every night, they can order in.

―――

The Virus Hits Home

Back in the UK, a loved one catches Covid-19 from a colleague in the NHS hospital where they both work. In Victoria, hospitals have pandemic protocols put in place to protect their staff. I'm aghast that the hospitals in England are failing to keep the infection under control. It's no surprise that this health worker takes Covid-19 home and infects her partner.

It's a scary feeling to be on a video call with someone who has always been healthy and see them coughing and looking frail. Her partner became so ill, she tells us, she called an ambulance, but the crew decided not to take him to hospital.

That night, his condition deteriorates. Scared that the ambulance won't make it in time, our loved one is forced to get into the car and drive 26 miles to the hospital. At A&E, she can't get the patient out of the car without assistance, and she calls for help. He is admitted immediately, sent to intensive care and given the same treatment as the Prime Minister, Boris Johnson. Half a world away in Melbourne, we are powerless to help.

It's moments like these you really do feel the tyranny of distance.

Before we left the UK, we had the not very cheerful conversation that five years is a long time to be abroad, especially when we have older family members, and we had to be prepared for serious illness, or worse. What neither of us could have predicted was the closure of Australia's international borders when the worst did happen. Not just once, but twice, we weren't able to be there in person to mourn with our family.

⌐⌐

The Weird World of Hotel Quarantine

Australia's mandatory hotel quarantine for international travellers comes into force on 28 March 2020. Passengers are met at the airport by Border Force officials, tested for Covid-19, and then escorted through immigration and arrivals to waiting coaches. All the passengers testing positive are put on one coach and sent to what becomes known as the "hot hotel". Everyone else is randomly assigned to a hotel in the city, all of which have switched from hosting leisure travellers to becoming isolation centres. They just have to hope that they'll get lucky and score one of the five-star hotels, instead of a Holiday Inn, Mercure or Novotel.

Hotel quarantine becomes a 14-day prison sentence as none of the hotel rooms have windows that open. At his five-star hotel, one traveller posts on social media that his reception committee consisted of police officers, members of the armed forces and hotel staff. There may be no locks on the doors, but there is CCTV, and when a "guest" opens his door to take a photograph, he gets a swift call from reception reminding him of the rules.

Anyone travelling to Australia during the pandemic is doing so for reasons such as returning home, relocating, taking up a job offer or visiting dying relatives. It's parents I feel most sorry for, as they must keep their children confined to one room and entertained for two weeks. I don't know how you could turn that experience into a game without going stir-crazy.

—

After 43 Days, Freedom

On 13 May, lockdown ceases. I'm desperate to get out of the city. Of all the things I miss from my old life, horse riding, my favourite hobby, tops the list. I took it up again after a long break once we moved to the countryside in 2011.

I find a riding school up by the international airport and it looks like I can get most of the way on public transport. It will still be a three-and-a-half hour round trip, on a tram, bus, and then a cab.

As the airport bus comes to a stop at Tullamarine, I spot a swarm of health officials in hazmat suits herding masked-up passengers onto coaches. Where is the money coming from to pay for the compulsory quarantine? For now, it's the Australian taxpayer. The hotels, most of which are global chains, must be laughing all the way to the bank.

I'm so happy to escape the grim reality of Covid-19 up at the stables but given how long it takes me to get there and back, it won't be feasible to ride every week. I get a lift with a woman who is trying out the stables as a one-off with her daughter and who lives in the city. She drops me off at a tram stop.

The lockdown respite coincides with both my birthday and our 20th wedding anniversary. Restaurants with outdoor seating are allowed to reopen, providing patrons sit outside.

Even though it's late autumn and cool enough for jackets and sweaters, BB Lookalike and I celebrate my birthday over brunch with family. And for our wedding anniversary, we buy a dressed Southern rock lobster, or crayfish as they're known here. But as Australia is being punished by China, which has banned their importation in a trade war, we get it at a discount, $100 instead of 130. It's an expensive treat, no question, but we get four meals out of one lobster and it's still cheaper than a night out at a restaurant.

Observing these milestones is a way to keep our spirits up as lockdown has taken its toll on both of us. It has been especially hard on BB Lookalike. He is still reeling from the announcement by Prime Minister Scott Morrison back in April when he held a press conference to advise temporary visa holders, including 500,000 international students, to return to their home countries if they couldn't support themselves.

'He's telling these kids that we're more than happy to take their money, but when the chips are down, they're not wanted here,' he said at the time. It's sad enough that the students lose out on the in-person campus experience, but if they do heed the advice, they won't be getting any refunds off the universities as the semester has started. Students who have already left and live in countries with censorship restrictions are reporting problems downloading the films BB Lookalike has set for them. These admin headaches are hard enough to deal with, but the fallout from the Prime Minister's comments makes BB Lookalike's already difficult job harder still.

'Imagine if he said that to the wine industry. There'd be an uproar. He doesn't have a clue how valuable higher education is to the economy,' he says. (According to a report by Deloitte, the Australian university sector in 2018 was worth $31 billion and employed 186,500 people full time.)

Alas, after eight weeks and four days of respite, one of the security guards working at a "hot hotel," passes Covid-19 on to his community, after which the Victorian Premier announces a second lockdown. If we think we had it bad during the first one, we ain't seen nothing yet.

This one lasts for 112 days and breaks a record as the world's longest continuous lockdown.

4

The Second Lockdown and Beyond

The collapse of the hotel quarantine scheme highlights how hollow it was to pretend that holiday destinations could turn themselves into medical facilities. How anyone in authority expected hotel staff, on minimum wage, with no medical training, to provide a safe and infection-free environment, I'll never know.

The Victorian government takes emergency action and bans all international flight arrivals from 10 July as it deals with the second wave of the virus. The Liberal opposition blames the Premier, Daniel Andrews, for the outbreak and demands that someone must take responsibility. Journalists from Rupert Murdoch's Sky News and The Australian fire question after question at the Premier, who is now so used to their antics, he acts as if he's made of Teflon.

Not So Civil Disobedience
As the second lockdown again makes us prisoners in our own homes, some people become rather less co-operative.

Anti-lockdown protestors go on social media and use encrypted messaging apps to organise mass rallies. Mostly fuelled by overseas-based conspiracy groups such as QAnon, they flood Twitter with false information.

Even here in St Kilda, we aren't immune from it. One day, when we leave our apartment building for our daily walk, a passerby stops us. She points to the mobile phone mast on the roof.

'It's really ugly, isn't it?' I say.

'You know who put it there, don't you?' the woman replies.

We nod our heads. 'Optus,' we say, naming the Australian telecommunications company.

'Nah,' she says, looking surprised at our naivety. 'It was Bill Gates. So he can spy on us. The government's locking us up so he can put trackable microchips in all of us. There isn't a virus.'

If a nerdy-looking man in glasses, a buttoned-down shirt and chinos was climbing on our roof, don't you think we'd have noticed?

I don't say any of this to the woman. Instead, 'How's he going to do that?' I ask.

'With the vaccine.' The woman's top lip curls and she gives me the side-eye—a look that says, are you really that stupid? We grin at her before hurriedly crossing the road.

'What is it about us and conspiracy theorists?' I ask. 'She's up there with Hans from Innsbruck who regaled us with his schtick about the Lizard People.'

'At least we weren't stuck on a minibus for two hours with this latest one,' BB Lookalike replies. (You'll find that story in Book 1, *The Accidental Plus One: Travel Tales from a Trailing Spouse.*)

On 20 October 2020, 107 days since the start of Lockdown 2, hundreds of anti-lockdown protestors hijack the Shrine of Remembrance, Victoria's national memorial, meant to be a place of quiet reflection to honour the sacrifice and service of Australians in war. As the demonstration turns violent, the protestors are confronted by police officers armed with pepper spray, tasers and a firearm. One of the low-lifes takes his anger out on the police horses and tries to hit their muzzles with a flagpole, but they are saved by their protective shields.

Three police officers are injured, with one admitted to hospital. Sixteen protestors are arrested with 96 penalty notices issued. The protestors score a spectacular own goal, alienating most Australians by their violent and abhorrent behaviour at the memorial.

When St Kilda becomes the next location for lockdown protestors to gather illegally, the police, who monitor all the social media channels, including the encrypted ones, are one step ahead of them. Two days after the ugly confrontation at the war memorial, police set up roadblocks early on Saturday morning. And then the police horse boxes arrive and park in the Palais Theatre carpark, just across the road. As a few dozen protestors gather on the St Kilda foreshore, they are vastly outnumbered by the authorities. During the clashes, a number of protestors are arrested but the protest is quickly dispersed. The mounted unit return to the carpark and the police horses are loaded into the horse boxes.

I hope they get the rest of the day off.

The mounted unit often patrols the beach and the foreshore as a peacekeeping initiative, and on hot days, I watch them take their horses down to the sea at low tide and allow them to splash around in the water. And the bond between horse and rider shines through. It's touching to see them at play, after all the violent demonstrations they have had to endure.

Ghost Town

In September, I was due for a dental check-up and a hygienist visit. I can't believe, as I write this now, that I was looking forward to it. So desperate to escape the monotony of lockdown, I was prepared to endure 45 minutes of the hygienist's ultrasonic scaler, if it got me out of the house and away from my same old routine.

So, let's go back in time to that day. On the 96 tram, masked up, I sit at least 1.5 metres away from the handful of fellow passengers. They must be essential workers, I guess, as all the offices and retail stores are still closed. As we pass the shuttered Crown Casino complex, in normal times a glittering temple to capitalism, it is eerily deserted, resembling the set of an end-of-the-world disaster movie.

The Southern Cross railway station, another place typically teeming with people on a weekday, is deserted as well. On Bourke Street, the only traffic we meet is construction vehicles. Construction is an industry that appears to be thriving in the city centre as on four different street corners, large-scale blocks are being built.

With next to no traffic, we reach Bourke Street Mall in record time. As I have half an hour to get to the dentist, I walk the rest of the way.

After crossing Swanston Street, I walk the two blocks to Collins. Out of habit, I press the button for the pedestrian lights, but there is no traffic, so I jaywalk across.

I couldn't get away with that normally, but what's normal these days? I ask myself. Deep in thought, I head up the hill in the direction of the Old Treasury Building, which sits at the top of Collins Street. During the Gold Rush era in the 1860s, this landmark held the original vaults of gold bullion, without which there would be no city to call itself "Marvellous Melbourne".

If you are going to flaunt your wealth, this is the place to do it.

But on this day, as I walk up Melbourne's answer to the Champs-Élysées, it is more menacing than marvellous. In a designer shop, the very tall female mannequins, painted a shade of alabaster, appear to look directly at me. They are each holding a large Max Mara carrier bag and standing in front of signs announcing that the brand's New Collection and Sale continues inside. Except, of course, that it doesn't, as the shop has been emptied of all its valuable clothing, no doubt removed to a warehouse for safekeeping.

And at the Gucci shop, which on any given working day would expect to have a line of tourists snaking around the corner, it's the same. All the other famous brands with shops on Collins Street are the same, populated by nothing more than naked mannequins.

Where hundreds of workers would generally be milling around outside or eating at the ground floor cafes at 101 Collins Street, one of the top corporate addresses in the city, it is like a ghost town. Everyone employed at the 57-storey office building, home to banks, financial service companies and law firms, is working from home. I can't help thinking of a "day the world ended" episode of *Doctor Who*. Any minute, I expect a parade of Daleks to appear, waving their gun sticks and screeching threats of extermination, followed by an army of Cybermen, firing their lasers in every direction.

That would have been a valid reason not to make my dental appointment, but I am already there, right outside the building. I put my mask on and make my way into the lift after smearing my hands with sanitiser. All the staff are masked up, but it feels reassuring to have other people to talk to. Even though the hygienist spends ages drilling the outline of every tooth with her de-scaler.

The Norfolk Island Pine Tree
I won't pretend that the 112 days of the second lockdown don't get me down. I crave nature and the solace of peace and quiet in the countryside, so I turn to what nature I have on my doorstep.

Outside our kitchen window is a giant Norfolk Island pine tree. Ten-storeys, it must be at least 30 metres tall. I don't know how old it is, but given that these trees are slow growing, it must have been at least fifty when the block was built in the early 1960s. I call it our wonky tree, as it has an alarming lean to about half-way up, where it started to grow straight. Battered by the prevailing southerlies, from the street, it looks like the Leaning Tower of Pisa. Passers-by pose in front of it for selfies. The tree functions as our privacy screen, partly shielding us from the block of flats next door, and it will be even more important when the new St Moritz development is completed.

I'm so grateful to have greenery to look at when I'm in the kitchen. At dusk, the tree is full of rainbow lorikeets cheerfully calling out to each other. The bolder ones make the leap onto our narrow windowsill, hoping to be fed, but as their new perch makes it impossible to open the kitchen window, they're out of luck.

'No, I don't have any food for you,' I say. They chirrup back at me, ever hopeful, even hopping along the sill so that they can get a better look at me washing up. They're such sweet birds.

They eventually give up and fly back to the tree, where there are tasty seeds for them to eat. Other visitors include ravens, mynahs and sulphur-crested cockatoos. I enjoy the birds' chatter, even the clamour of the cockatoos. In the absence of being able to socialise with my friends and family, these beautiful creatures provide a colourful and cheerful alternative. Their conversation is somewhat limited, though, so I do still crave the day when the world begins to open up again.

Elwood Sourdough

As well as enjoying the wildlife on our doorstep, getting out and about is another panacea to soothe our souls in this most difficult of times. One of the regular walks we started in the first lockdown takes us along the waterfront from St Kilda, then turns inland via the Elwood Canal to complete a circular loop back to the St Kilda shops.

The canal was built on swampland and it's neither fragrant nor very attractive, but it's a pleasant enough place to stroll as there's a shared paved footpath and cycle path on both sides. As we are heading east one day, walking along the left-hand side of the canal, we notice a long line of people queuing up outside what appears to be someone's house. We spot a trestle table set up with baked goods and a cheery woman in bright coloured clothes is serving customers.

This being lockdown, we have to keep a metre and a half away from the next person in the queue. But we need bread so buy a sourdough loaf from the cheery vendor. Which sweet treat to choose proves more difficult.

All the baked items have names. The currant buns are Spotties and the walnut shortbread with salted caramel is a Lochie. I choose the latter and, after one bite, vow to recreate it in my home kitchen back in Winchester one day, when Melbourne is but a distant memory.

This woman isn't merely running a pop-up bakery business—it's her passion. So much love and enthusiasm have gone into the preparation and presentation of her food. Who knew that buying bread could be so uplifting? And what a community asset to have in lockdown. Her quirky boutique offerings have won her many fans; some of whom are willing to walk to their entire 5k limit just so they can buy her bread.

Mean Girls

BB Lookalike and I celebrate the end of lockdown with a barbecue, inviting a handful of friends as a gradual reintroduction into society after 112 days of mostly socialising online. On 9 November, I mark the reopening of gyms and libraries by booking my first exercise class and borrowing a pile of books. Although it's still six weeks away, I even start planning for Christmas.

With the easing of restrictions, households are permitted to have 30 people in total on Christmas Day. I find this amusing as I don't even know 28 people in Australia. We will be a table of four (five if you count a canine guest) on the big day, but even though the numbers may be small, I still want to make it a day to remember.

In preparation for the imminent reopening of my gym, I pack up all the weights I borrowed into the shopping trolley that was so handy 112 long days ago and, with the help of BB Lookalike, deliver them back across the road. As the classes are reinstated, it feels great to be able to work out with other people. But I've been back barely a week when something happens that rather takes the shine off it.

I walk into my gym class, put my bag down and set up my equipment, as is my habit. However, when I go to fetch my weights and return to my spot, I am accosted by a small middle-aged blonde woman.

'You can't go there,' she barks, baring her even white teeth. Her lips are plumped, and she has neither laughter lines nor wrinkles. It's an expensive face I'm looking at. I guess by her tiny physique she was probably once a gymnast or a jockey.

I look around the studio to check if anyone else has heard what she said, but the only other person is her side-kick, a tall, perfectly toned ash blonde, a dead ringer for *Absolutely Fabulous*'s Patsy Stone. She is wearing sunglasses —indoors. But it's her scowl that is the giveaway—she has "model" written all over her.

I've made the rookie mistake of being alone in a room with someone not only spoiling for a fight over territory, but who has brought a stand-over woman with her. Mature and subtle me would observe Tiny Diva's intimidating behaviour and reflect this back to her calmly and confidently, avoiding emotion. Today, I am neither mature nor subtle.

'I don't see a reserved sign, maybe you should get here earlier if you want to bag a space.'

'I've been standing in that spot for the past twenty years,' Tiny Diva says. I try not to laugh as I picture her leaving an armed guard in place while she nips to the loo.

You need to get out more, I think, stalling for time. It's still only me in this room with this girl gang, so I have no back-up. If Tiny Diva is telling the truth, she isn't going to give up one inch of her territory.

I stand my ground. She flounces off, tossing her long bleached mane and muttering to Patsy. They huddle together like teenage Snapchat addicts, throwing me evils every now and again.

Imagine going to the same school as those two.

When the instructor comes into the studio, Tiny Diva is all over her. As my punishment, when she puts her equipment away, she "accidentally" drops a weight right next to my bench, while I'm lying on the floor. To everyone else in the room it would look like an accident, only I know it wasn't.

And this isn't an end to it. Another time, I set my bench up and go to fetch my bag. As soon as my back is turned, Patsy comes striding into the studio, sunglasses still on. In the mirror I see her kick my bench, which goes flying. She then proceeds to set up her own step where my bench once was.

She recognises me. Maybe it's revenge for standing up to Tiny Diva.

But even I'm not prepared to take on someone this angry before breakfast. The two others in the room busy themselves staring into their phones.

I'm not the only victim. A classmate puts the fan on ten minutes into the workout when Tiny Diva interrupts the class by turning it off, because *she's* cold. The instructor is caught off-guard by the control freak's antics.

After the class, when Tiny Diva and Patsy have flounced off to be anything but absolutely fabulous somewhere else, a few of us stay to discuss a strategy to deal with her bad behaviour. When I have related my experiences to other gym friends, they've told me they've either been on the receiving end of Tiny Diva's vitriol, or watched her try to intimidate fellow gym goers. This bullying needs to stop!

For a while after this, I manage to avoid the woman as we come to classes at different times, until she turns up one Thursday morning. There's a 15-minute window between one class finishing and the next starting. Those of us about to work out line up politely, waiting for the last class to leave. All except for Tiny Diva, who barges in and sets herself up in her usual place. I stand away from her, behind two gym members who are friendly, and beside the victim that triggered her most recent meltdown.

Unfortunately, the Tiny Diva school of bad behaviour seems to be catching on. One morning, a friend spots what she assumes is a free bench, right in front of the offending fan. But as she goes to set up her weights, a newbie marches in and barks at her.

'What do you think you're doing?' she screeches. 'That's my bench. I put it out before the earlier class.'

'I asked the instructor who said it was free,' my friend says.

'Yeah, well he's wrong,' the woman replies, all huffy and aggressive. As my friend tries to diffuse the situation in a calm and polite way, Tiny Diva walks in.

'You stand your ground,' she says to the newbie. 'You were there first.'

All this drama and it's not even 8am.

What the newbie doesn't realise is that she's right in front of the fan. And when another member switches it on, for a moment, it looks like she's about to complain. Then she thinks better of it and puts on a sweatshirt.

Much as it's nice to be working out with my friends again, I have to say we didn't have all this aggro during virtual gym in lockdown.

Unwanted Visitors

In early December, before I put the finishing touches to the Christmas plans and read through turkey recipes, I have a more pressing avian problem to deal with. On a warm morning, I wake up early, eager to greet the day, and unlock the balcony door next to our bedroom.

'Coo-coo, cheep-cheep.' I go to shoo away the pigeons. But I don't see any. One of my other senses is assaulted, though—there's an overpowering smell of uric acid and excrement.

'Eurggh. I'm going to have to clean up after them now.' I slam the balcony door shut but leave the window open. The birds sound like they're in the room with us. There's no respite from the coo-cooing and cheep-cheeping.

'They can't even keep time,' I complain as a chorus of coo-coos starts up, each bird a jarring split second out of sync with the rest of the choir.

'Who can't?' BB Lookalike asks.

'These smelly invisible pigeons.'

I look down at my lack of clothing. If I am going to be playing Miss Marple, I'd better cover up. I don't want the neighbours seeing me like this. I grab my dressing gown, wrap it around me and tiptoe out onto the balcony.

The cooing and cheeping get louder. I look up, expecting to see the birds on the roof, but the sound seems to be coming from underneath me. Holding my nose because of the ammonia stench, I peer over the balcony to see if they're on the floor below, but the cheeping is too close for that.

'They might be inside the air-conditioning unit,' I call to BB Lookalike. 'Maybe there's a hole in it and they crawled in.' But as I examine the unit from the front, there's no visible sign of entry. Puzzled by this, I peer around the back to see if they got in that way. Staring right back at me are two beady black eyes. A pigeon is sitting on a nest. A nest with broken shells. And not only that, a nest full of live chicks. I count four.

'Oh God. This is worse than I thought,' I say, going back into the bedroom and pulling the door shut.

'What is?' BB Lookalike asks. I can't bring myself to tell him what I've seen.

'Take a look for yourself.'

He gets up, goes onto the balcony and peers around the back of the air-conditioning unit.

'I see what you mean,' he says when he returns. Then he goes back to reading his book.

I sigh. 'What do we do?' I ask him.' It's a family of baby pigeons. I can't bring myself to evict them from the nest.'

'We could wait until they fledge, then get rid of the nest,' BB Lookalike says. He doesn't seem to be taking this seriously.

'How long is that going to take? And what if it gets hot and we want to put the air-con on?'

'Then they'll be keener to move out,' he says.

'We'll probably end up with some horrible lung condition from breathing in their droppings,' I mutter as I go online. 'It takes four weeks for them to fledge,' I tell BB Lookalike as I google baby pigeons. 'We might have to move out.'

Every day, I peer at the nest, staring at the pigeons.

'You lot better be out of here by the time we go to Tassie, or there'll be trouble,' I tell them. 'And keep the noise down over Christmas. If Betty finds out you're here, it's curtains.'

'Coo-coo, cheep-cheep,' they answer. I neglect to tell them that Betty is a Schnoodle. They'll be able to work that out for themselves if I forget to close the balcony door.

In the countdown to Christmas, I pretend the pigeon family doesn't exist. For Christmas lunch, we will start with cream cheese and lumpfish caviar blinis, followed by Samin

Nostrat's butterflied turkey marinaded in buttermilk, which keeps the bird beautifully succulent. The sides are to be roast potatoes, cashew and cranberry stuffing, gravy, asparagus and toasted almonds, with a tomato, goat's cheese and green salad. And for dessert, Nigella Lawson's chocolate pavlova with berries.

We are grateful for a scaled-back Christmas as in the days leading up to it, we receive tragic news that a beloved family member is dying in the UK. As we are still cut off from the other side of the world, we are distraught when on 27 December, our relative dies.

The next few days go past in a blur as we try to process our grief. We spend New Year's Eve with local friends a little way outside of St Kilda, which will be party central. While we are grieving, neither of us has any enthusiasm for partying. The support from these friends and family in Australia keeps us going.

We do have some distractions from our grief. As well as our upcoming trip to walk the Bay of Fires in Tasmania, we still haven't figured out how to solve the pigeon problem. Over the next few days, the temperatures hover around the mid-twenties. Despite us hoping for a heatwave, the weather won't play ball.

Finally, the last of the pigeon chicks fledges. I pick up the now empty nest, wearing heavy duty gloves, ready to throw it away. And then I notice something wriggling. The nest is alive with mites. But to get rid of it, I have to bring it inside.

I can't risk it. I'll throw the abandoned nest over the balcony, but I can't do that in daylight in case someone sees me, or I accidentally hit someone in the carpark below. I wait until nightfall, which in the summer isn't until after 9.30pm. I do a quick scan of the carpark, nine floors below. The coast is clear, so I fling the nest as far away from the parked cars as I can manage.

But that night, I can't sleep. I toss and turn. I'm itchy, but it's not mosquitos.

'Are you being bitten?' I ask BB Lookalike.

'No,' he says, before rolling over and falling asleep. I want to turn on my reading light but get up instead and run to the bathroom to examine my skin.

Little red mites crawl up my arm. And more are probably crawling around in the bedsheets. I jump in the shower and wash my hair, not caring that it's the middle of the night. I am awake until morning. By 8am, I'm calling a pest control company. The clock is ticking as we are flying to Tasmania in two days.

'I'll come tomorrow,' the pest control agent says, 'but you'll have to close the bedroom doors while the spray takes effect.'

'That's fine. We're going away.'

I force myself to go back into our bedroom to retrieve my clothes. The thought of sleeping in there while we still have mites makes me gag. I'm not sure how long they've been there, but the infestation could have started when I picked up the nest or when the chicks were waiting to fledge.

We decamp to the guest room. Because of the lockdowns, it has so far hosted no guests, and the only times we've used this bedroom are when one of us has been sick or can't sleep.

Where are we going to go if we have an infestation in here as well? I ask myself. I pull back the sheets and inspect the bed for the tell-tale little wriggling red dots. I get the magnifying glass to make sure. There appear to be none.

I breathe a sigh of relief as we'll be safe from them in

here. As a precaution, I throw all the clothes I was wearing when I hurled the nest over the balcony into the washing machine, along with the linen from our bedroom, and put it on a hot wash. Then I go online to find two bug-proof mattress protectors. I order them and hope they will have turned up by the time we come back from Tassie.

We spend a comfortable night in the spare room, with the window open. It's far away enough from the air-conditioning unit that any stray mites would have trouble crawling in. And when I wake up, I'm bite free.

That's one problem resolved, or at least in hand. But in between packing for our trip, I fret about how we're going to stop the blasted pigeons from returning every time they want to raise a new brood.

BB Lookalike comes up with a suggestion. 'We could put something behind the air-conditioner that would make for a very uncomfortable nesting experience.'

'Like a hawk?' I say.

'I was thinking of rocks.'

'There aren't any on our beach that we could carry. It's either sand or boulders. There's no in-between.'

I make another phone call. Our pest control agent suggests bird spikes and drops them off when he comes to apply the spray. When I show them to BB Lookalike, he comments that they're made of plastic.

'We can't put those behind the air-conditioner, they'd melt as soon as we turned the unit on,' he says. 'What else can we use?'

Empty jars and wine bottles is the simple answer. I gather as many empties as I can find and shove them behind the unit, then I switch on winter followed by summer mode. Neither spark nor smoke comes out of the unit, which is a good sign. It looks like the bottles and jars solution will work perfectly for the next four-and-a-half years until we vacate the premises.

All I will have to do is remember to recycle the bottles before the letting agency's final inspection.

5

Finding Freedom in the Bay of Fires

My fixation with the rainbow lorikeets in the wonky tree was my way of saying I was missing being amongst nature during lockdown. Confined to home, I'd become an avid armchair traveller and loved hearing about other people's adventures. When a newspaper columnist raved about the Bay of Fires guided walk, a trip she took between lockdowns, I jumped online.

The Bay of Fires is a 50km stretch of beach located on Tasmania's remote northeast coast and is mostly national park. The trip, run by the Tasmanian Walking Company, is a luxury three-day jaunt and costs $5,500 for both of us. That's nearly two economy airfares back to the UK. But as there's no realistic chance of a return to the UK in the foreseeable future, while the borders are sealed and the planes mothballed, why not, we decided, use the money set aside for this year's long-haul travel on a trip of a lifetime?

Qantas doesn't even have any long-haul aircraft onshore; they've all been moved to storage facilities in deserts across the world. And its long-haul cabin crew have either been furloughed or have found new jobs. Our local supermarket is currently employing three of them, including the manager, who tells me the horror stories of what it's like to deal with the verbal abuse of demanding passengers at the pointy end of the plane.

Fortunately for us, domestic routes between cities are still running, but with far fewer planes than normal. On top of the money I've set aside for the walk, I cost out the prices of the extras I'll need to add on. Return airfares for two to Launceston at $288, a night in a hotel before the trip and one night after. Entally Lodge, 11km outside of Launceston in the countryside, is where we are to be collected at 7.30am the morning after our arrival. With a discount offered through the Tasmanian Walking Company, bed and breakfast costs $159. I find a better deal for our last night on 12 January at the Hotel Grand Chancellor in town for two, $20 cheaper, including breakfast.

I booked the trip and paid the $1,000 deposit in September 2020, while we were still in the second lockdown. The booking form states that the trip is fully refundable should we be unable to go because of coronavirus restrictions. Tasmania has different rules from Victoria and the Covid situation changes day-to-day.

I made the final payment for the full amount in December when we had come out of lockdown. I read the small print and knew we would be required to buy specific clothing for the walk. The kit list is so comprehensive, it reminded me of the school uniforms that my parents were forced to buy when my sister and I were boarders at the Holy Family Convent in Littlehampton, England. I didn't factor the hiking gear into my budget as it will come in useful for other walks.

My daily 10,000 steps on the flat weren't going to be any match for the distances we would be expected to cover on the trip, but at least it was better than nothing. Since booking, I'd been nervous about the second day as it's 14km across soft sand. Having paid the balance, I set my misgivings aside as there was still plenty that could go wrong over the next few weeks, the main one being a sudden return to lockdown in Victoria or Tasmania.

I don't sleep too well in the nights leading up to the trip as I'm so excited. Two days before departure, we fill out the paperwork, a mandatory travel declaration to give to the Tasmanian State Government. The main proviso is that our Covid-19 vaccination certificates are up to date. I have these stored digitally in my Apple Wallet. Our paperwork takes less than 24-hours to process and we are good to go.

As the plane rumbles down the runway at Tullamarine, I can scarcely believe that we are finally able to go away on holiday, after all these lockdowns. In less than an hour we arrive in Launceston. We are greeted by a big, burly Immigration Officer as well as a Department of Health Officer. As a precaution, I kept a paper copy of the digital forms we filled in. I pass our paperwork over to the officials, confident that this is just a formality. But the Health Officer shakes his head.

'You'll have to fill in a new form for both of you. This is out of date,' he says, handing me back my paperwork.

'But it's only two days ago I filed it and got accepted. Here's the screenshot I took,' I say.

The Officer gives a shrug. 'It's your bad luck the rules changed half an hour ago.'

While we were mid-air!

He softens his stance. 'You'll be alright as long as you both fill in the forms. You've travelled from Victoria. If you were coming from Queensland, that would be a different story.'

I don't dare ask him what he intends to do with Queenslanders. I'm just happy that we've had a narrow escape.

Tasmania, here we come!

Arachnophobia!

The next morning we're up bright and early, and are ready by 7.30, even though our official meeting time is eight. The Tasmanian Walking Company office is abuzz with travellers, most of whom are being kitted out to do the Overland Track, a long-distance hike across the mountainous interior. So far, we appear to be the only takers for the Bay of Fires.

At the last-minute, a woman carrying a smart camera joins us. She is both an artist and photographer and we rejoice as we couldn't ask for a better walking companion. It was meant to be a group of thirteen, but ten of the walkers have the misfortune of coming from Queensland and are forced into hotel quarantine. Our guides, Ben and Dan, tell us there will only be the five of us on the walk. Two guides for three hikers! What a luxury.

We unpack our walking gear and lodge wear and put them into the waterproof day packs we're given, which we must carry. They warned us not to take more than 9kg each. I weighed my gear before we left home, but didn't factor in the heavy duty raincoat that the company provides and insists we take, even though no rain is forecast for the entire trip. Not only is it heavy, it's also bulky, but it's a deal-breaker as they won't accept alternatives.

But given the amount of equipment that the guides are having to take, which includes a packed lunch for each of us as well as the ingredients, drinks and miscellaneous items for dinner and breakfast, it looks like we got off lightly.

Our group set off in the company Land Rover and head inland towards the north-east coast, stopping off in the former tin mining town of Derby for a coffee and a comfort break. The town has reinvented itself as the top Tasmanian destination for adrenaline-junkies, and it's teeming with thrill-seeking mountain-bikers, who whizz along the trails that run adjacent to the main road.

After Derby, it's late morning when we arrive at Stumpy's Bay, Mt William National Park, and the start of the walk. There's a group photo and then it's time for the off. It's mid-20s and there's a cooling breeze, ideal walking conditions. I inhale the pure air, so glad we're doing this. On a day like this, you can see all the way across the Bass Strait to Flinders Island.

Today's walk is billed as an easy 9km and should take us no more than four hours. We cross a long sandy stretch to Boulder Point. Our guides suggest walking on the packed sand closest to the shoreline, rather than further up the beach where it's softer. It's good advice. With the wind whipping the words out of our mouths, we walk along in companionable silence.

At Boulder Point Ben and Dan lay out a picnic lunch of ham and cheese sandwiches, fruit and homemade cookies. The two lads get out the billy and rustle us up a cup of tea, accompanied by more delicious homemade biscuits.

If I keep eating like this, I'll be one of the few long-distance walkers to gain weight.

We reach Foresters Beach Camp at 4.30pm. It's tucked away from the beach in secluded dunes, out of the wind. Our rooms are timber-floored and housed in semi-permanent tents, with canvas rooves. Inside there are two beds on wooden slats and the mattresses are about six inches thick and covered in a waterproof coating. We are each given a sleeping bag. I try out my bed. It seems cosy enough, if a little hard.

The camp is connected by wooden boardwalks, with the tents at one end, nearest the beach, a deck with a wooden table in the middle, and behind that a full kitchen, where the guys are already hard at work preparing our three-course meal. At the back is the toilet block with sinks and pristine composting loos. It's been very well thought out to have minimum environmental impact.

'Let's go for a swim,' BB Lookalike says.

'You're on.'

Getting into our swimmers is the easy part. As we walk along the boardwalk towards the beach, we stop, taking in the silver sands and the glacier-blue water. From one end of the pristine beach to the other there isn't another soul around.

'There's nothing between us and Antarctica,' I say, dipping my toes into the icy water. 'If we want to keep clean, we're going to have to go for it as we won't get a shower until tomorrow night.' BB Lookalike looks doubtful, hanging back. I start to run as the water gets colder. I'm up to my waist but can't bring myself to take the final leap as it's heart-stoppingly cold.

'You wouldn't think that in high summer it would be this cold, would you?' I say, bobbing up and down in the water and making a half-hearted attempt to wash.

'It's Tasmania.'

Enough said.

I race back up the beach, shivering, and grab my towel. Walking back to camp, the smell of something delicious that the boys have cooked up wafts in our direction. It's time to change into our "lodge gear", even though we're going to be dining outside under the stars.

While Dan is putting the final touches to our starters, Ben is acting as maître d'.

'What would you like, red or white?' he asks, indicating the bottles of local wine he has opened. We opt for red to warm us up after our swim, plus it will help me get to sleep. The wine, like everything so far on this trip, is top notch.

What could be nicer than sitting on the deck, in the middle of nowhere, eating our way through a delicious three-course meal. These guides work their socks off. Not only do they have to be gourmet cooks and excellent travel guides, getting us safely along the track in all weathers, they also need to be trained first aiders. If one of us were to have an accident or get bitten by a snake, we will be in good hands.

Once it's dark, it's time to turn in. I've been putting this bit off, but as I glance around, all I can think of is how many big spiders have got into my sleeping bag while we were at dinner. I put that thought aside until I return from the bathroom block. Then I unzip my sleeping bag, directing my head torch towards every crease and seam. I give it a good shake. Meanwhile, BB Lookalike has climbed straight into his sleeping bag, without so much as a glance at its contents, and is already sound asleep.

I lie down on my bed and try to read my Kindle for a bit, using my head torch to give a better light than the backlit screen. After about half an hour I give up and turn it off. And lie awake for what seems like the whole night. By 2am, I'm in urgent need of the bathroom, but the thought of venturing into the wilderness puts me off. It is something I'm going to have to work up to.

I unzip my sleeping bag, find my flip-flops, grab the head torch and venture cautiously down the boardwalk. I don't switch the torch on as I don't want to wake any of the others, and besides, the moonlight and the stars are ablaze. Suddenly there's a loud thump next to me, which scares the bejesus out of me. Then a large, hairy thing brushes past me, nearly shoving me off the elevated walkway and onto the sand below.

Wallaby. Phiff. Not scared of those.

As I get to the bathroom, which is pitch black, I stick the headtorch on. If there is anything lurking, it's going to be in here. I do a spider audit of my cubicle before using it. Hopefully, I can make it back to our tent without being knocked to the ground by a large bouncing marsupial.

I lie awake for the next couple of hours, waiting for the sky to lighten. By the time it does, BB Lookalike is awake, so we go down to the beach to watch the sun as it comes up over the east coast.

'Another swim before breakfast?' I ask.

'I'll wait for it to warm up first,' BB Lookalike says. At breakfast, I down copious cups of tea, before Ben comes out with our omelettes. As he places our plates in front of us, he looks embarrassed.

'I'm sorry about the huntsman,' he says, referring to Australia's very own breed of spider the size of a tarantula.

'What huntsman?' I blurt out.

'The one in the toilet block,' Ben says. 'I've moved him on now.'

'I got up in the middle of the night and checked out the first bathroom and there was no sign of one.'

'It must be your lucky day as he was in the second bathroom.'

'There is a God, then,' I say, tucking into my delicious breakfast. 'I hope you relocated him far enough away that he won't find his way back. At least not before we leave.'

The Tough Route to Heaven

Sunday 10 January is the longest walk of the trip at 14km. This doesn't sound like much as it's mostly on the flat and I've done distances of up to 25km before now, but I have been apprehensive about this day for a while. As soon as we start to walk and our feet sink into the sand, I realise why. The softer the surface, the harder it's going to be to lift one foot after another, especially when we've been walking all day. And to cap it all, the mercury is predicted to soar to a very uncharacteristic (for Tasmania) temperature of 33 degrees. I felt the 9kg pack resting on my shoulders yesterday, but today it feels like a lead weight.

The instructions were to dress with our swimmers on underneath our clothes today as the guys predict that part of the track will have been washed out because of recent rain and we'll likely have to wade across water. It takes just over an hour to arrive at Deep Creek. Dan and Ben get on their two-way radio to consult colleagues about where the best crossing point will be. After about ten minutes, they come back with the plan.

'We're going to wade across the creek,' says Dan. 'Ben is going first to make sure it's not too deep for the rest of us to follow. If he can make it across without falling in, he'll wait at the other side. Then we can pass all our gear overhead, so that it doesn't get wet.'

I'm going to get that dip after all. I hope the creek isn't as cold as the sea.

I peel off my our outer layers until all that's left is my swimmers. Ben sets off and we watch him make his way, one step at a time.

'What are you walking on, rocks or sand?' Dan asks.

'Sand,' Ben shouts back. That's a relief, as I forgot to pack my waterproof shoes.

He makes it across and we all clap. And then he

returns, helps Dan ensure that all the luggage is sealed, and crosses once more to the other side of the creek, while we gather at the edge, ready to start sending the gear across.

And then we notice something curious. So much for being out in the wilderness, with no one else around. Staring at us from a holiday house, barely 50 metres away, are around a dozen people. They have a dingy with an outboard motor, I note, which could ferry our gear across the creek or, better still, drop it around the headland in five seconds flat. But they'd rather gawp at us, like we're the morning's entertainment, than offer to help. I expect they're hoping that one of us townies from the mainland is going to lose our footing and fall in the creek.

I'll show you.

'I'll go next,' I call out and make my way confidently to the water. I brace myself for the cold, but the creek water is as warm as a bath. And it's just flowed past that holiday house full of smug onlookers. I hate to think what's in it. I set the thoughts of effluent aside and I'm across the creek before I know it, silly grin on my face.

I take my place in line, ready for the rest of the team to start handing over the gear. When the holidaymakers notice that we've managed to get ourselves and all our hiking kit across without any mishaps, they turn away, disappointed.

Better luck with the next group of hikers, I think.

On the other side of the creek are some handy boulders where we change back into our hiking gear. We drape our swimmers and towels over our backpacks to air as we walk along. By the time we reach our lunch spot near Eddystone Point lighthouse, they're dry. My feet are boiling hot in my hiking boots and thick socks, and so are everyone else's by the look of it, as we all pull our footwear off and fling it aside on the rocks. We paddle up to our ankles along the translucent shallows, walking across the silver sands that stretch down to the line of gently curving cobalt-blue waves, 50 metres away.

After our paddle, we wade back, tired toes loving their bathe. I'm not looking forward to pulling my boots back on, so I distract myself by piling into the ham and cheese sandwiches which the boys made first thing this morning. They hand out fruit and more homemade biscuits.

'Who makes the biscuits?' I ask. 'They're delicious.'

'The lodge chef. But if you think these are good, wait until you see what he's preparing for tonight.'

'I'll hold onto that thought,' I say as I reluctantly dry my sore feet, put my thick woolly socks back on and stand up. BB Lookalike helps me on with my pack.

Barely halfway and I'm already shattered. But I'm egged on by the experience of being in this pristine environment. The colour contrast between the blue of the sea and the rocks we changed behind is astounding. The rocks are granite and covered in bright orange lichen. I assume that these flame-coloured rocks are why the area is called the Bay of Fires.

It turns out I'm wrong.

When the east coast of Tasmania, or Van Diemen's Land as it was called in 1773, was charted by Captain Furneaux, his sailors observed a string of fires along the shoreline, lit by local Aboriginal people. He was observing a practice for managing the landscape that had—and has —been ongoing for thousands of years.

I scan the endless stretch of beach. There are rocks dotted along the way and as we walk, it requires some scrambling. It's not exactly elegant, but I manage to get up the rocks with the help of BB Lookalike shoving me from behind.

'This is the exact halfway point and we only have another 7km to go,' Ben calls out.

Blimey, I hope I can manage it.

After the rock scramble, the way ahead is pristine beach. I plonk myself on the sand, pull off my boots and socks and walk along the shoreline barefoot, bathed by the incoming tide. By 3.30pm, we're making our way along deserted beaches that stretch as far as the eye can see.

Ben draws our attention to a range of hills in the distance. 'The lodge is up there,' he says. My heart sinks. The views must be stunning from that vantage point, but at the end of a tough 13km in 33C, we have at least another 1km climb with 9kg packs to carry. By now I'm on automatic pilot, putting one foot in front of the other.

At least once we start the climb, we'll be in shade, I tell myself. As we ascend, the weight on my back seems to get heavier. I am halfway up the hill when I can go no further.

'I'll leave my pack here and come back for it later,' I say to BB Lookalike.

'No,' he replies. 'I'll carry it.'

'You can't lug 18kg up a hill like this. We'll take it in turns,' I say. And so we make our way up the hill, one step at a time, with BB Lookalike doing most of the heavy lifting. As a distraction, by this point I'm counting steps. At around 500 steps, the scent of pine wafting through the air eggs me on.

Just a few more, I tell myself, until the tracks turns into wooden steps. We make a beeline for the benches laid out near the entrance to the lodge. We take off our boots and are ushered to the back deck. Laid out for us are foot spas with running water. I fling off my socks, roll up my walking trousers and dunk my sore feet into the warm water. I'd *almost* do the walk again, just for this. I shut my eyes and fall back into my chair.

'Champagne?'

Could it get any better than this? I think. The Chef/Manager of the lodge is there with a tray of drinks in his hand. I take a sip.

'I'm going to have to get a photo of that bottle,' I say. 'It's heavenly.'

'Glad you like it, it's Clover Hill Vintage Brut, as served at Princess Mary's wedding.' That would be Tassie's home-grown princess, Mary Donaldson, now married to Prince Fredrik of Denmark, no less.

Princess Mary has good taste. No wonder I like it so much.

The euphoria from two glasses of champagne and a foot spa weaves its magic on all three of us as we lose track of time. After we've all had a good soak, we take in our surroundings. There is an outdoor tub, but we forgo that for our first hot shower in two days. Although I could sit here all evening, I reluctantly haul myself out of my chair.

It's only as I make my way along the corridor to where our luggage is parked that I begin to appreciate the open aspect of our digs for the next two nights. Our room is Scandi-style minimalism, warm-toned wood and glass louvres that open out onto the bushland. I can't wait to be lulled to sleep in a proper bed, with the wind whistling through the she-oaks and the sound of the waves crashing along the shoreline far below.

Once we've changed, we make our way into the lounge area, which overlooks the open plan kitchen where the Chef/Lodge Manager is busy putting the finishing touches to tonight's dinner. Our guides were right. If we were impressed by their efforts in the camp, Chef has gone all out this evening with a three-course meal accompanied by a selection of Tasmanian wines.

That's followed by a briefing from the guides about the next day's activity, which to my relief is a six-hour adventure, but one that involves plenty of sitting down as it's a combination of kayaking and walking. The briefing is rudely interrupted by banging and crashing in amongst the trees. We rush over just in time to see a mob of kangaroos who seem in a tearing hurry to get somewhere.

As day becomes night, we look up to a million twinkling stars. This is one magical holiday.

From Lockdown to Lifelong Memories

The next morning we're treated to a breakfast of scrambled eggs, toast, fresh fruit, juice, coffee and pastries. I ponder the logistics of getting fresh food supplies into what is a remote national park. There's a 4WD parked around the back of the lodge, which must have to bump along the dirt track firebreaks until it reaches a sealed road. Then it has a further hike to the nearest town, St Helens. If by chance you forget something, you can't exactly get a food delivery app to bring it to you out here.

BB Lookalike, Lucy the artist and photographer and I set off on our walk at 8.30am, this time with a considerably lighter load as we are returning to the lodge for our final night. We are accompanied only by Ben because Dan will meet us with the Land Rover to drive us to the start of our kayaking trip.

This will be the fourth time I've kayaked and I'd like to say that I've got better at it, but that would be a lie. On each occasion, when BB Lookalike and I have shared a kayak, we have spent most of our time bickering about which oar to push off on, Or, worse still, we've just gone around in circles. That was all very well on the kayaking equivalent of nursery slopes, the lagoon in Rarotonga, which at its deepest was four feet. We tipped upside down a couple of times, but there it didn't matter.

This trip, we are going to be travelling along a gently flowing river, which will be deep, so we'd better get our act together. After donning lifejackets, we are given a quick refresher course in the quieter part of the river. I'm relieved that the kayaks are the sit-inside type which are more stable. I'm at the front and BB Lookalike is at the back.

I dip my finger into the river and pull it straight out again. It's icy. I may be an okay swimmer, but I sure as heck don't fancy hauling myself back into the kayak if I fall in.

Dan travels in the same kayak as Lucy, and Ben, as tour leader, is in a single kayak. BB Lookalike and I glide down the river, the current doing most of the work. It's so peaceful and tranquil, I hope the others don't hear us muttering to each other.

'Dip the left oar into the water, as otherwise we won't go straight,' BB Lookalike mutters.

'I'm trying to.' It's trickier than it looks as somehow, we have to master matching our strokes. Apart from kayaking trips, the only other time we argue is on long car journeys following unfamiliar directions.

Just then, BB Lookalike's hat goes flying off and lands in the water.

'We're going to have to go back for it,' I say. Ben, who is right at the front, hears me and turns around.

'I'll get it for you,' he says.

He's seen what a pair of incompetent idiots we are.

Once Ben has kindly retrieved BB Lookalike's hat, we proceed down the river, again letting the current do all the work.

I'm starting to get the hang of this.

We even master the slow stop, when Dan points to a clump of tall trees. At the very top is a vast nest, with a giant sea-eagle perched in it. We watch on, mesmerised.

Around the next curve in the river is open water up ahead as it flows out into the bay. There's a fresh breeze and the water ruffles up. The boys offer up two options: kayaking across the bay to a distant headland, or the easier option, a paddle around the edges before lunch. The bay from this angle looks benign enough, but looks can be deceptive, and after a quick show of hands, we choose the shorter trip.

Lunch is a picnic, for which the guys have once again pulled out all the stops, with the additional help from our lodge host. The leftover seafood from last night's dinner has been repurposed and turned into wraps and sand-wiches. And afterwards, there's fresh fruit and yet more homemade biscuits. Luckily, we still have a couple of hours walking left to burn off all that yummy food.

Then it's back to the lodge, our home away from home, for one more night. And after our solar powered showers and a change into our lodge gear, we make our way out to the front deck, with its sweeping views of the Tasman Sea and our bush surroundings in the national park. As we are settling in with another glass of local wine and some pre-dinner nibbles, below us comes the sound of voices and trudging feet. And before we know it a group of ten walkers arrive and plonk their packs down before heading out to the foot spa.

By the time dinner is ready, our quiet little party of three has grown to thirteen and the atmosphere has turned up to maximum volume as the group—colleagues who work together in health—are celebrating a big birthday or two. The self-proclaimed Brisbane Ten were booked on our walk, but got detained at Launceston Airport and had to go into hotel quarantine for three nights while the Tasmanian health authorities decided whether to send them back or allow them in. If I was in their shoes, I'd be wanting to let off steam too.

By 9.30pm someone has cranked up the music and is singing along, and I know I'll regret it tomorrow morning if I don't make my excuses and head to bed. I whisper to BB Lookalike and we get up and bid the assembled guests goodnight. Our room is at the back of the lodge, away from the yoga room where the group has retreated to. Whether they've run out of steam or been asked to keep it down, I don't know, but not long after we leave, the music stops.

The next morning the Brisbane Ten wander into breakfast, bright-eyed and bushy-tailed, which is remarkable, given the copious amounts of alcohol they consumed last night. We are going our separate ways today, as it is our last day here.

As we pack up our gear and say goodbye to our host, we take in the stunning view for one last time, before we follow our guides to the back of the lodge and set off on our hike. It's the easiest day of all today as the walk is an hour at most. But as we make our way through the coastal heathland and the eucalypts, Ben signals to us to stop. Then he beckons us over.

Curled up and looking like it's asleep is a tiger snake. These snakes are highly venomous, so we give it plenty of space to move away, but it doesn't seem too bothered about our presence. BB Lookalike and I are familiar with this breed of snake from when we lived close to a water bird sanctuary in Melbourne's west. In hot weather, they used to sun themselves on the shared walking and bike path. We soon learnt to get out the way when the "large stick" blocking our path started to slither.

After our close encounter with Tasmanian wildlife, we have lunch then walk towards the pick-up point where the minibus is waiting to take us back to the real world. Returning our backpacks to Entally Lodge and repacking our suitcases, we then have a celebratory glass of bubbles with our tour guides before heading off into Launceston for our stay at a city hotel. While I'm living in Australia, for every celebratory occasion, the bubbly will have to be Clover Hill vintage.

We truly have had an experience that we'll remember for the rest of our lives, which we'd never have done had it not been for lockdown. Thank you, Covid!

6

From Comfort Cake to Fine Dining

As I'm a seasoned comfort eater who uses food as a way of dealing with difficult emotions, it wasn't all that surprising that in lockdown, eating became a solace. I developed the habit as a young child at boarding school when food was a coping mechanism if I felt homesick. The one item we could bring from home was a tuck box, the contents of which were meant to last until at least half-term, when if we were lucky, we could get a refill.

Mine consisted of chocolate and butterscotch. I liked to bite into my Lindt animals and then let the milk chocolate melt on my tongue. Then I'd move on to the Callard & Bowser butterscotch. The packets were white and soft, and the pieces were rectangular and wrapped in shiny gold foil. They looked like smaller versions of the gold cigarette boxes that grown-ups bought.

While other bored foodies nurtured sourdough starters and spent lockdown perfecting bread baking, I bailed on this one, because within what was then our permitted 5km radius were so many bakeries, I'd stopped counting. As well as the established ones (three in St Kilda, three in

Balaklava and two in Ripponlea), a pop-up bakeshop began trending on Instagram. This wasn't any old bakeshop, but a genius re-set for the closest Melbourne has to the legendary Noma in Denmark or a Fat Duck in England.

Attica, a boldly ambitious, innovative temple to gastronomy, revered by chefs and foodies the world over, had to close its doors during lockdown. The restaurant not only lost all its income overnight but had the added responsibility of trying to save the jobs of its staff. The Attica team, headed up by chef and proprietor Ben Shewry, announced that while the restaurant might be closed, they'd still be in the hospitality business, converting the premises to a temporary bakeshop. As word got out on Instagram that the acclaimed chef and his team had pivoted to producing affordable baked goods, foodies within the permitted 5km radius rejoiced. At last, we had a chance to taste the *Chef-du-Jour*'s cooking, without having to re-mortgage the house to afford a multi-course degustation menu, which with matching wines would set us back over $1,000 for two.

On the menu were Attica's most popular items, including Vegemite scrolls and the team's twist on the iconic Aussie chocolate bar, a Cherry Ripe. These populist offerings were embraced by those of us in the neighbour-hood. Not only did I live within the regulation 5km, but so did my only Melbourne-based family members, who love all things Attica. We agreed to split the cost of whatever was still available by the time one of us was able to hot foot it to Ripponlea and wait in the long line. We would then arrange a socially distanced meeting on a street corner (we weren't allowed to mix and mingle with another house-hold) and divvy up the goods.

If I was lucky enough to catch a post about the

bakeshop the night before a pop-up, I could co-ordinate my visit to coincide with opening time. But even then, other locals always got there before me. It didn't matter. The anticipation that I was going to walk home with delicious baked goods to share out was all I was interested in. The pandemic might be hell, but at least there was cake! And what I was here for *was* cake. Cheesecake—not a regular baked or cold biscuit-based dessert, but a speciality Basque cheesecake, as served in the town of San Sebastian in Spain.

The queue for the bakeshop generally stretched all the way down Glen Eira Road, with each person waiting in line wearing a mask and standing the regulation 1.5 metres away from the next person. When in position, I would send a photo to my relative to show her where I was in the queue. As I got closer, I'd feel a sense of camaraderie. We had all been lured here by the promise of foodie treats, and if standing in a line was the closest we were allowed to get to socialising, we'd take it.

Soon, there were only four customers in front of me. I listened out for their orders. Vegemite scrolls and cheesecake were the requests on everyone's lips.

Please let there be some cheesecake left, I thought.

At last it was my turn. The person serving me had dark curly hair and kind eyes above his mask. I was sure it was the main man himself. Flustered, I homed in on the vegemite scrolls but my eyes were fixed on the cheesecake. I ordered both.

The cheesecake was modest in size but must be mega-rich as it was meant to serve eight. And at $70 a pop or $35 for four servings, it was a luxury. But an affordable one, at least then, when going out to restaurants was not an option for the foreseeable future.

I sent a text with a photo of the cheesecake fix I'd

scored, arranged a rendezvous for later on the street corner outside our apartment. Now I had to walk the cheesecake home, avoiding all obstacles and anyone who might knock me over—pedestrians and all the food delivery drivers who would insist on riding on the pavement.

Once safely home, I cut the cake in half, put it on a plate, covered it loosely and placed it in the fridge. Because BB Lookalike was in his office on Zoom and I was in the kitchen alone, I wiped my finger along the flat blade of the knife and tasted the leftover cheesecake from it.

Wow! I could see what the fuss was all about. But how was I going to hold off devouring a slice right now? I didn't see how we'd get four portions out of this.

I cut out two slices carefully. And as I have no self-control, I went in with a fork and started my portion. So much for saving it for dessert. *But this is research*, I told myself. I took small mouthfuls, lifting the fork with one hand, pen in the other as I noted down the ingredients. Eggs—mostly yolks, judging by the golden colour. Sugar, cream (more than one type) as well as cream cheese. The only other flavour I could detect was vanilla.

Let's not pretend that this is in any way healthy, I thought, shovelling in another mouthful.

Cheesecake Obsessions

That evening, after we've both devoured our rations, I go online to find a Basque Cheesecake recipe. I am expecting it to have been passed down over the genera-tions, with a long history attached. But as far as prove-nance goes, it's only as ancient as shoulder pads and big hair. In the 1980s, Santiago Rivera, chef/owner of La Viña, a bar-restaurant in San Sebastián, must have been bored, as he challenged himself to make a new dessert every day.

He came up with this one, featuring cream cheese, not an ingredient traditionally associated with Spanish desserts. What sets Burnt Basque Cheesecake apart from the pale American-style ones is that there is no pastry or biscuit layer. Instead, it is a rustic-looking dish with a caramelised top. It contains just five ingredients and is easy to make. What's more, the pastry chef has been generous enough to share his recipe online and you can find it at: https://span ishsabores.com/burnt-basque-cheesecake-recipe/

In lockdown, my obsession for creating the perfect Basque Cheesecake kicks in. But when I make the dish using the original recipe, it tastes different to the Attica one. And because this is lockdown and life as we know it has changed and my world has shrunk, I obsess about how the recipe has been adapted.

It dawns on me that it must be something to do with the cream. The American expression "heavy cream" (a thick liquid-based cream) doesn't easily translate to Australia. There's "pure cream", which is liquid but not thick, and then there is double cream, which is very thick. The product known as "thickened cream" is manufactured, bulked out with added gelatine. I avoid thickened cream, especially if I'm having vegetarians over for dinner, who won't want cartilage, skin and animal bones in their dessert. In the EU, New Zealand and the UK, cream can't, by law, be made of anything other than milk from an animal.

Chefs constantly tweak recipes and I imagine that at Attica, it's no different. Since this is 2021, and social media have gone crazy for Burnt Basque Cheesecake, there are as many variants of it as there are Instagram hashtags. When I get bored with trawling through these, I decide to extend my cheesecake repertoire. One of our local bakers, Darren Purchese of "cake studio" Burch & Purchese, offers cook-along classes over Zoom on a Sunday afternoon during lockdown, and I can't think of a better distraction on a winter's day than making cheesecake with a maestro. And we get a free digital recipe book, *Cheesecakes, Baked, Set & Whipped*, by Darren Purchese thrown in.

With my newfound enthusiasm for all things cheese-cake, I make as many different ones as there are days in the month. We do not, I hasten to add, devour these all ourselves. I use them as currency to barter for food with family members who live within my bubble.

Not content with making Darren's recipes, I order BB Lookalike's birthday cake from the man himself in September 2021, when we are still in lockdown. As BB Lookalike is working from home, I have zero opportunity to hide a homemade birthday cake from him. And I can't exactly nip around to a friend's house to bake and decorate one as we aren't allowed in anyone else's home. To mark the occasion, I order a round "Flavours of Peach Melba" birthday cake with a personalised chocolate plaque saying "Happy Birthday, BB Lookalike" on it.

I travel to South Yarra, on the outer limits of my 5km zone, to get the delicate cake. I then have to transport it home without dropping it. But the cake—an airy feather-light concoction with the delicate taste of peach, is so deli-cious, we are bereft when it is finished.

Evil Genius

As well as the perfect Burnt Basque Cheesecake, Attica adds another dessert to its bakeshop repertoire called Evil Genius. By looking at the cake, I can see it has a white sponge layer (probably vanilla) topped with a molten caramel sauce that oozes butterscotch. I imagine it tastes just like the Callard & Bowser butterscotch from my childhood.

I put my spoon through the two layers, then separate them out. The sponge is indeed vanilla, but I'm not sure whether it's an angel cake or an all-butter variety. And the sauce tastes of butter and sugar, certainly more butter-scotch than caramel. After eating the two together, I need to lie down.

What I can't work out is how to cook this without the top layer oozing through to the sponge. I am not, I decide, going to attempt to recreate this cake and will just have to keep it as a food memory.

Bored with cakes, I turn my attention to cocktails. These are the stuff of the celebrations, drinks parties and social events that we are currently banned from hosting, so a cocktail isn't the kind of drink I can justify having on my own. Nonetheless, while idly scrolling through my *New York Times* recipe app, searching for something quick to make for dinner, I stumble upon a recipe for turning fresh cherries into alcohol-infused cocktail snacks.

The recipe involves both the cherries and a bottle of Maraschino, a fiery-tasting unsweetened spirit. I buy the bottle and sit it unopened at the back of the spirits cupboard, where it waits for four months until cherry season in January.

By the time the cherries are at their peak in the Southern Hemisphere, rather than waste them on cock-tails, I perfect a black forest cake and a trifle using the liqueur. The bottle lasts us for another three years post lockdown, by which time I've lost count of the number of boozy cakes I must have made.

Although lockdown is now a distant memory, I am still

a fan of Attica, subscribing to the team's emails and following them on social media. And it's there I read a post headed "Evil Genius Recipe". The genius bit is that it's a cake baked in two parts, with the vanilla sponge baked first, then left to cool. The topping is a blondie mixture, spooned on top of the sponge and baked for a further 45 minutes. And in case you want to try it for yourself, here is the recipe: https://www.attica.com.au/attica-digest/recipe-the-evil-genius.

A Taste of Heaven

Although I've been able to replicate the Evil Genius recipe and it reminds me of the best of lockdown, by March 2025, I am yet to step over the threshold of Attica's restaurant. I can't think of any occasion that would justify $1,000 for two for dinner.

But all that changes when I open my Attica newsletter and up pops an initiative called "Snacks With…" This is a series of wine pairings and snacks, each night hosted by a different staff member. I message my regular dining companions, offering up a couple of dates in June. They give me an enthusiastic yes and, in my excitement, I… manage to screw up the booking. The restaurant team gets back to me, pointing out that I've booked two separate tables. No, I tell them, I didn't intend that two couples sit at opposite ends of the dining room, waving to each other.

Prior to arriving for our booking, all we know is that we aren't getting a full meal as our slot is just an hour and a half. That may sound like plenty of time to eat dinner, but there is, I hope, going to be some theatre involved. We also have no idea how much we are going to be charged. But one thing's for sure, it will be a unique way for BB Lookalike and me to bookend our five-and-a-half years in Melbourne.

Two days before our booking, Attica contacts us via the OpenTable app to confirm. I attempt to ask how much it's going to cost but I don't get a straight answer. We can choose food off the à la carte menu, the team member tells me, and it depends on what we order. They send a link to the sample menu, which consists of small plates of a few bites of food, carefully curated to show off the cooking skills of the chef. I pick up that there is kangaroo, crustacean and a mushroom dish, all of which I will happily eat.

I seek answers online and find a helpful Reddit thread. Saltwater Souva is a playful interpretation of souvlaki, a favourite dish of Australians of Greek heritage. Only Attica's version consists of saltwater crocodile, desert lime, Geraldton wax and macadamia yogurt. It may indeed be a "unique culinary experience," but as I was pressured into trying chewy and salty alligator at a work dinner in the USA, I will pass on this one. An additional item on the menu is emu, a large flightless indigenous bird, distantly related to a chicken. As there are at least 630,000 of them in the wild, they are certainly free range. I worry, though, that the meat might be tough as emus can run up to 50km an hour, especially when someone wants to catch them for dinner.

As some of the courses are interactive, including one that involves a tour through an art installation in the garden, I don't think that we snackers will be afforded the theatrics, but I'm still hopeful.

After further online research, I find out that the event will be held in Attica's wine bar, rather than in the main dining room. I didn't know the restaurant had room for a wine bar. Is this place built like a Tardis, big on the inside but small on the outside? So small, in fact, that when I whizzed past in a bus just yesterday, I blinked and I missed it. Then I note Attica's Head Sommelier will be featuring a selection of rare and interesting wines to pair with these snacks.

Fabbo, that's what we're coming for, I think.

And now for the snacks: 'The à la carte menu will change for each session, so expect a different selection each time.' At previous events, diners have been served a selection of the following:

'Fried Mussel Gildas: A classic Spanish snack with a twist, featuring fried mussels'. 'Kangaroo Tartare with Macadamia Puree: A more adventurous option showcasing Australian ingredients'. I hope that this is on the menu as you can't get more Aussie than that. 'Ben's Family Lasagne: A popular dish known for its rich béchamel and garlic bread'. During lockdown when Attica was a bakeshop, I bought the lasagne dish as it was included in a three-course meal option. It was so delicious that I was hanging out for the recipe for ages. Ben credits his mother Kay Shewry for the original recipe and I finally found it as it was featured on the radio in New Zealand. I make the lasagne whenever I go to visit one branch of my family. It is a cinch to make and the bolognaise sauce component is so delicious that it even gets the thumbs-up from a six-year-old. Okay, she has hers with plain spaghetti, but still, I feel chipper about that.

As it's a special occasion, we get a lift to Ripponlea, an untrendy part of Melbourne 9km southeast of the CBD. It has a suburban vibe, but does have a direct train route into the city, and its main strip, Glen Eira Road, has excellent food shopping and eateries, with Attica as its star.

When we arrive, we are ushered into the bar area, passing one of the restaurants on our left where diners appear to be eating the full menu. The building is indeed much bigger on the inside than it looks from the street. The bar is to our left, and beyond that is a large round table that has yet to be set. We are offered seats at this table.

As soon as we sit down, we hear what we think at first is chanting coming from the kitchen. Is it some kind of team bonding exercise? I ask the friendly waiter, who brings our starters, to tell us.

"Oui, Chef," she replies with the traditional response to the Head Chef's instructions to make sure the kitchen brigade have understood the orders. Only in French. Of course it would be. It's Attica.

What we don't know about our table, until we have had a drink and our first snack, is that we are sitting in the middle of a four-way intersection or roundabout. I am facing one of the two dining rooms, a Zen-like space which gives off a serene, tranquil vibe. Guests eat off different crockery and drink from jewel-coloured glassware. Attending to their every need is a dedicated wait staff team who observe proceedings from a servery, linking this small dining room with the kitchen—the engine room of the restaurant. The food for these guests is served from a cross between a trolley and a high-tech version of a Lazy Susan.

To the right of me is the kitchen where our snacks come from, and behind that, past the bathrooms, is another kitchen, which I'm guessing is the pastry section. I enjoy being in the centre of everything, as I can watch the comings and goings of the dozens of wait staff, sommeliers and managers. The servers wear utilitarian khaki-coloured collarless shirts with grey pants, which make them all look like Communist Party officials.

As we are handed our menus and drinks list, another server comes around with tap water. The floor manager who escorted us to our table says that she will give us a few minutes to read the menu, and then spoils it by reminding us that we've got to be out in an hour and a half.

Yes, we get it.

We had a message from OpenTable only yesterday, after I'd confirmed our booking, telling us that: *"Tables are reserved from the time you've booked for one and a half hours"*. That's hardly the relaxed and informal "wine bar" experience we were promised, but we do what we're told and choose quickly. There's a slight confusion with the wine order but a quick swap between two of us sorts this out.

So, what do we end up eating?

A generous chunk of sourdough bread with cultured butter, which is both delicious and a bargain at $8. One of our crew has a cheese puff with wattle miso cream for $6. Despite being a forlorn, anaemic-looking bun on a plate, it turns out to be sensational. I'm not game (see what I did there?) to order for myself a whole portion of emu liver parfait, which is so rich, it's enough for four of us to share. The parfait is a slab on the top of melba-like toast, served on a wooden base to elevate it. It is decorated with dots of Ooray (Davidson's Plum) jelly as an homage to 1970s chicken liver paté. This is also six bucks.

My starter is char-grilled roo skewer in a mountain pepper satay. Cooked perfectly, medium rare, it tastes like it's just come off the barbecue. Delicious. I pass two little pieces of fillet for the others to try. For my main course, I choose the crispy prawn open sandwich. The prawn is big and juicy, the size of a small marron, and the bread is a soft white disc, Japanese-style, with a smear of mayonnaise on top.

None of us has room for the sea bounty mussels and local greens, nor the whole grilled flathead in seaweed butter and native herb sauce, the most expensive item on the menu at $55. The standout dish of the day has to be the warrigal greens, black ant (yes) and banksia cheese toastie, served with a bush tomato soup dip. Never in my life have I eaten a better cheese toastie. The black ant tastes like a little citrus pop on my tongue.

We share two portions of hand-cut chips with Attica tomato sauce between the four of us. They are proper chips, twice fried. The portions are large even for two and we have some left over. To finish, we share fresh Long Paddock cheese, again deciding on two portions. This is like ricotta, served with slow roasted quince, which is delicious and perfectly balances the cheese. The wattle crackers remind me of a tastier version of communion wafers.

As the evening is as much about the wine pairings as it is the food, I feign an interest in the two named winemakers. Patrick Sullivan is Mr Chardonnay and William Downie the pinot noir man. I choose a Black Sands 2024 chardonnay from Heywood in Henty, 33 km west of Melbourne on the Bass Coast, not because I know anything about the wine, but for its price. It's the cheapest glass on the list at $24. For the cheese course I opt for a glass of Gippsland 2024, also at the same price. Although I've heard of Gippsland as an emerging wine region, Heywood is new to me. My adventurous dining buddies choose a glass of the more expensive wine.

During the evening, the great man himself comes out from the kitchen to greet a guest at the bar. I look up and observe that he is very tanned. Maybe he doesn't spend every day and evening slaving away at the stove.

The next day I get a message from OpenTable, asking for a review. I give the experience four-and-a-half stars out of five, the half point deducted for the awkward reminder the moment we sat down that we were on borrowed time. The irony was that during the cheese course, one of the charming wait staff told us to take our time as the table wasn't needed again after all.

I will always be grateful that we finally got to dine in at Attica. We didn't come for the bragging rights—to be able to say we've eaten at the best restaurant in Australia—but to remind ourselves how much of a part Attica played in helping us survive lockdown. And, of course, to celebrate that we have since come full circle.

7

Cabin Fever

One of my many distractions in lockdown was to stare wistfully at our garden back in England via the home security app on my phone. So when, two-and-a-half years after we left, I finally get to go back home, I can scarcely believe it.

I'm so out of practice with long-haul flying, I have to relearn how to pack. I'm booked on the shortest route—Melbourne-Perth-London—on Qantas. It's four hours to Perth, then a whopping 17 hours non-stop to Heathrow. It's 4C when I wake up on 1 June 2022 and 10C when I step into the taxi. I'm wearing thermal layers that I can peel off and a lightweight trench coat, which I pack into my suitcase on arrival at Tullamarine airport.

I won't need that in the terminal building, I tell myself. But once I'm through security airside, I can't get warm, especially when I walk past the bank of draughty windows in international departures.

An hour before boarding is due to commence, I bag myself a seat at the gate. Then as more passengers appear, I overhear a conversation that the inbound flight from

Perth is delayed. I get up and look at the departure board, but it still says we are due to leave on time mid-afternoon. Then, via the Qantas app, I receive a text message, telling me that our flight will be delayed by two hours. It's annoying, but I'm not going to let it rile me.

What's an extra two hours after two-and-a-half years?

I get up and go for a brisk walk as, despite my layers, I'm still feeling distinctly cold and am regretting ditching my coat. Two hours become three, four, five and then six, when we are finally told that there is a mechanical problem with our plane. It requires a spare part which is being flown in from what I guess to be Singapore as our flight is delayed a total of 11 hours.

As every hour passes, I get colder and more shivery. And no matter where I sit, I can't seem to get warm.

But one of my layers is cashmere, so what's going on?

At 6pm, the passengers from our flight are called to the check-in desk and given a food voucher of $20 each.

What an insult.

If this had happened in Europe or the UK, we'd be entitled to some serious compensation.

Resigned to the delay, I take my $20 voucher and go in search of somewhere I can spend it. I head for the airport pub because at least I can get a glass of wine. I order the wine and present my voucher, only to be told that it isn't redeemable against alcohol. I will have to buy something to eat. None of the food appeals, as it mostly involves hot chips. The smallest item on the menu is nachos with cheese and sour cream, which is not something I'd normally order as they sound very rich, but I figure they'll soak up the booze. And as we could be waiting a long time for this spare part to turn up, it's probably better to have something now than at three in the morning.

Maybe I should have trusted my instincts. Almost as

soon as I've finished my glass of wine and the plate of nachos, I feel violently ill. And I get sicker and more shivery as the night wears on. I am so desperate that I text a friend with Qantas Gold status to see if she can comp me in the Qantas Lounge. Unfortunately, for some reason, this doesn't work and I'm denied access. I just want to curl up in a ball, I'm feeling so bad. I take two paracetamols but they have no effect.

At 2am our flight is called and I finally sit down in my seat. But as soon as I do, I feel sick. I call the crew, who take one look at my ashen face and usher me down to the back of the plane. They ask me my age and start giving me oxygen as they think I'm having a heart attack. I suck in the cool air and am enjoying the sensation when I see the doors are about to close so we can get on our way. I go back to my seat and sit down.

I'll have another 21 hours of this. What would happen if I could only make it as far as Perth? I don't want to force the crew to look after a sick passenger, so I put my hand up and ask to be let off the plane.

The captain, who has been delayed for the same length of time as his passengers and is in danger of going over his hours, is kindness itself. He announces that there will be a further 45-minute delay before the plane can set off on the four-hour journey to Perth. I'm too ill to feel sorry for my fellow passengers, even though I'm the one causing the hold-up while the baggage handlers try to find and offload my case.

A member of ground staff is waiting for me on the airbridge and escorts me back through security. The Border Force officers take one look at my puce-coloured face and shaking body and stand back, in the manner of the parting of the Red Sea. Even though I'm at death's door, I can appreciate that there can't be many people who have had the experience of going through security the wrong way. I'm then taken downstairs to arrivals where I wait for another 45 minutes for my bag. Once I have it, I wait still longer for the promised airport car, which never arrives. I make my way to the taxi stand. Luckily I'm the only passenger waiting in line.

By now it's 4am and I have been at the airport for 15 hours. I should be somewhere over India, but I'm at ground level at Tullamarine. It's too early in the morning to text BB Lookalike as he'll still be asleep. And as I'm going to wake him anyway by returning at 4.45am, it's only fair he has as much sleep as he can get.

As I arrive in the apartment, he greets me at the bedroom door. He woke, he tells me, to the sound of my key in the door. I stumble towards him, mumbling that I'm very ill with some horrible bug, and put myself to sleep.

I am out for nearly twelve hours, sweating profusely. When I wake up, I feel light-headed. And this how it is for the next three days. I call my GP who says from the sound of the symptoms it could be Norovirus. And now I have passed it on to BB Lookalike. The GP tells me that the only thing we can take while the bug goes through our systems is paracetamol.

I'm still so weak that I haven't given a thought to rebooking my flight, but because of Covid, all air fares are fully flexible and I'm able to change without penalty. Unfortunately, there are no seats left on any of the Qantas flights via Perth in the foreseeable future, but there is a seat on its codeshare airline, Emirates, but via Dubai. The downside of the Emirates flight is that check-in is a hideous 4.15am with a departure at 6.15am. It's hard enough to sleep well the night before a long-haul flight, but having to get up at 3am to get to the airport is downright cruel.

As I voice my misgivings, the Emirates representative

offers me an upgrade to Premium Economy for an extra $600. As I'm still ill, I gratefully accept it. To mitigate the risk of getting a further food-borne virus, I ask for the special vegetarian meal. What I don't know is that most airlines don't differentiate between vegetarians and vegans, and my meal will, in fact, be plant-based.

Ah well, give me a vegan meal over norovirus any day.

Beans, Beans, Beans

With military-like precision, I am up and out the door and in the back of an Uber by 3.45am. The only traffic we encounter are taxis and trucks, and I'm dropped off at the airport with five minutes to spare before the official check-in time at 4.15am. I pat myself on the back, thinking I'm early. But there before me is a queue that snakes out the door of the terminal. I ask the people in front of me where they are going.

'Dubai. This is the line,' a woman barks. I scan the horizon for any sign of a separate check-in for Premium Economy. But it's only for First and Business Class.

It takes 45 minutes to get anywhere near check-in. The plane is an A380, at what looks like full capacity, which could be up to 500 passengers. No wonder it looks like chaos up ahead.

Nil points, Emirates, I think.

An hour before our scheduled departure, I start to relax as I watch my luggage disappear onto the conveyor belt. Once through security, I make my way to the gate. It's packed and there's not a seat to be had. I stand, waiting to be called. At least here, Premium Economy passengers get to board before the hordes.

My seat is an aisle one on the left-hand side of the aircraft, in a configuration of two. I say a silent thank you to the Emirates customer service help desk which got me this seat. For the next 14 hours, I can get up and walk around the cabin without having to crawl over anyone else. The seats are very comfortable and more like Business Class compared with Premium Economy seats on other airlines.

An hour after take-off, we are served breakfast. Normally I look forward to mealtimes on board planes as a way of distracting myself from clock-watching, but I haven't been the least bit hungry since I got sick. It's just as well, as the vegan breakfast put in front of me is a most unappetising portion of navy beans in a savoury sauce. They're not a patch on good old Heinz baked beans. Accompanying them is a dry white bread roll with vegan spread that looks so horrible, I can't even bring myself to try it. The second vegan meal is some sort of rice dish. It's still not that nice, but better than the beans I had earlier.

There's nothing Premium about the food, that's for sure, so I snuggle down in my seat, making myself as comfortable as I can. I manage to get a few hours' sleep. As we make our final approach to Dubai, out the window, it looks like a scene from a dystopian movie. There are dust storms swirling around, kicked up by the desert winds, and it's only at the last minute that I see the towering silver skyscrapers as they've been covered in a grainy fog. As I look down, it doesn't seem like this environmental disaster area could sustain anything.

As the aircraft heads towards the gate, the thick-set man in the aisle seat opposite me stands up and opens the overhead luggage bin right above my head. He is solidly built with a grim expression and not one of the crew challenges him, even though the plane is still moving. I wouldn't be game to tackle him either. As soon as the doors open when the flight stops at the gate, he pushes his way past all the other passengers to get to the front.

Good riddance, I hope he's connecting to somewhere other than London.

⸻

The Social Media Influencer

My transit time is 45 minutes and I join the queue for hand luggage screening, which airport security insists upon even for transit passengers. The queue is a long one and I'm desperate to find a pharmacy. I'm suffering from motion sickness but by the time I find one, buy the pills and the water to wash them down with, my flight is being called.

I'm one of the last remaining passengers to board. But as I sit down in my seat in Premium Economy, a young woman with long hair, flaunting her midriff in a skimpy flesh-toned Athleisure two-piece, walks past me, tossing her locks. Her leggings accentuate her curves but leave nothing to the imagination. Above her bare midriff are two conical boobs that threaten to burst out of her crop top. She reminds me of Barbie. Her accent, as she talks non-stop into her phone, sounds British.

'I'm on the plane in Emirates Premium Economy,' she chirps as she takes the seat in front of me. 'I'll show you around.' As she pans her phone camera around the cabin, I shrink down in my seat so that I'm out of shot.

She must be doing a paid promotion, I think. *Just my luck to be seated right behind an Instagram influencer.* Although her inane commentary is unlikely to result in other young women flocking to the United Arab Emirates in her footsteps. Not when they could go to Spain and flaunt their bits in public without running the risk of being arrested in a conservative country for looking like a stripper.

The other passengers in the cabin are a mixture of Westerners and couples from the Gulf States. Some of the local women are wearing hijabs, covering their heads and necks, and I spot at least two wearing niqabs, which cover their faces. I wonder how they feel about scantily clad Westerners strutting around their country, oblivious to the local customs.

We take off on time at 2.15pm. About half an hour into the flight, Miss Social Media pulls out her phone again.

'The crew are coming around asking me if I'd like a drink before the meal service and I've ordered an Aperol Spritz.'

She pans her camera towards the patient female flight attendant serving her, who plays along, smiling and waving to Miss Social Media's followers. But as I can't see from my seat what else is being filmed, I get up on the pretext of re-arranging my clothing. I time it just as Miss Social Media takes a photo of her bright orange cocktail.

Hashtag getting tipsy on the plane? Or how about, hashtag are you feeling jealous yet?

Once she's finished her drink and the crew have been to clear everything away, Miss Social Media gets up and walks around the Premium Economy cabin, filming indiscriminately. I choose now, between the drinks and the meal service, to get up and go to the bathroom, but am conscious I might end up on Instagram. Luckily, as I make my way back to my seat, Miss Social Media is forced to sit down as the crew are serving lunch. Or is it dinner? I can't tell.

'I'm choosing my meal and I don't know whether to have the chicken or the fish,' Miss Social Media says.

Paraphrasing the words of that famous Aussie songbird, Kylie Minogue, I think, *You should be so lucky. Don't mind me while I chow down on the exact same "special" beans in a red sauce I ate 16 hours ago.* I pick up my dry white bread roll and marvel at the way it crumbles in my hand. Do the crew have a special dehydrator that makes the bread rolls stale? Once again, I pass on the revolting vegan spread.

Thankfully, Miss Social Media runs out of steam quite soon after her meal.

Has she exhausted her material, run out of things to brag about? Perhaps the alcohol has gone to her head, but I don't hear another word out of her for the rest of the trip. However, right before landing, she gets up with her beauty case and trots off to the bathroom. She's gone for ages and when she comes back, she's layered the slap on so thick, it's hard to know where the real her begins and ends. Her foundation is an alarming shade of mud, and she's either managed to curl her eyelashes in the bathroom or attached fake ones. No wonder there was a long line of passengers queuing outside. I wonder what they thought of having to wait so long while she put on her face.

When we arrive at 8.15pm, I could kiss the ground as it's my first time back home in so long. I'm through security in half an hour. The Winchester taxi service I've booked is there, waiting to take me home.

Before I set off on the return journey in September, this time on Qantas, I manage to get through to the help line and cancel the special meals before I fly. As a result, my food selection is delicious and as I scan my fellow passengers, none of them appear to be "influencers". Nonetheless, for all my remaining long-haul flights between the UK and the Southern Hemisphere, I will switch allegiance from Qantas to Air New Zealand and Singapore Airlines.

When I walk past the pub at Tullamarine airport, the shutters are drawn as it's not yet opening time. Three years on, I still can't face a plate of nachos.

8

Strangers on a Train

Over Christmas 2022, on a family visit back to New Zealand we play tourist, swapping a plane for a slow train.

After a great night out with friends in Auckland, we're up bright and early the next morning, grabbing a takeaway coffee and croissant before catching a cab to a nondescript suburban railway station in Parnell, ten minutes away from town. There, waiting for us, is the Northern Explorer, a smart tourist train. Back in the day, we knew the service on this line as the bone shaker from Auckland to Wellington, to be avoided at all costs.

If you've ever fought your way onto an overcrowded train in Britain only to find your reserved seats occupied by the luggage of stroppy ladies returning to Birmingham from a cruise, the Northern Explorer is practically the Orient Express. We find our comfy seats, including head-rests, with our names on them, enough space to store luggage, oodles of leg room and a no-nonsense train manager. In my experience of commuting on British trains, at the first sign of aggro, the guard disappears. And who would blame them when Brummie women try it on with their guilt-tripping tactics?

'I want to cry,' one wailed on that fateful trip as we shoved their bags out the way and sat down in our allocated seats. I stared straight ahead. They were a gang of four opposite us and to the right, and spent the entire trip giving me evils.

If your luggage is so precious, I told them in my head, *put the cases on your own seats and you can stand. Or next time, how about taking a smaller suitcase?*

Another time, we witnessed an altercation when two young women boarded a delayed train that was so full, it was standing room only. As they made their way towards what they claimed were "their" booked seats, they discovered two other young women had already occupied them. As we were watching from the train platform, we couldn't hear the argument, but were able to watch their body language. The two women in the disputed seats pointed firmly to the reservations sign above them. If the system was working properly, it would have been easy enough to verify their claim to the seats, but the two who had just joined the train leant over them, arguing their case.

As the train left, half the passengers were still standing and would have to do so for the hour it would take to get to London. How ironic, then, that two minutes later, an identical London bound train, half empty, pulled up at the station. We were betting that the two young women had got it wrong and were booked on that train. They, and all the standing passengers that had crammed onto the delayed 16.33 service, could have had a comfortable journey if only they'd waited an extra two minutes.

The joys of train travel in the UK! As I glance up and down our carriage on the Northern Explorer, all is quiet. I silently rejoice that there is neither on-board wi-fi nor mobile phone coverage, so fingers crossed there won't be any kind of shenanigans on this train as we settle in for our 11 hour journey.

Facing the direction of travel, which is a relief, we introduce ourselves to the two Australian travellers seated opposite us. The train departs on time at 7.45am. As we glide out of Auckland, I fire up the audio commentary, detailing the history and background of the areas as we pass them. That this narration can manage to make suburban Auckland, a place I lived in for five years, interesting is no mean feat.

An hour into the journey, past the urban sprawl, we spot rolling hills and bush-clad countryside. We traverse the delightfully named Bombay Hills and there below, spread out before us, is the Waikato, a lush pastoral landscape punctured by volcanic peaks. We arrive in Hamilton two hours and twenty minutes after we left Auckland. It brings back memories of the first place we lived together in New Zealand when we moved here in 2000.

By 10am, after our early start, I'm gagging for a coffee. I get up to go to the cafe carriage, which comes with a proper espresso machine. Not only that, it has a dedicated seating area, so that you can dine in. It reminds me of the old-fashioned dining cars common on trains back in the day, which have nearly all disappeared in the UK.

I order two flat white coffees to go, then make my way back to my seat to find that the train manager has dropped off the menu for today's trip. It's Christmas themed, serving, amongst other dishes, turkey, stuffing and cranberry sandwiches as well as mince pies. These fruity pies are served at Christmas in the UK, Ireland, Australia and New Zealand, but are virtually unknown in the USA, as the word "mince" is associated with meat. At other times of the year, the Northern Explorer even serves their version of a cream tea, with scones, jam and cream.

The Tongariro Crossing

Both I and Mark Smith, who runs the website *The Man in Seat 61*, agree that the Northern Explorer is a must-do for visitors and locals alike. He goes further and says it's one of the top long-distance train trips in the world. I'm taking his word for it, especially as it even has an open viewing carriage. Make sure you've secured your spot before 12.20pm to experience the engineering feat known as the Raurimu spiral.

In rugged terrain, engineers solved the problem of getting up and down a steep slope without the need to build a network of extensive bridges. The Raurimu spiral is a track that loops back on itself, goes around in a circle, passes through two tunnels, and includes several sharp bends.

It's worth staying in the viewing carriage for the next spectacular attraction, Tongariro National Park, home to three volcanic mountains: Tongariro, Ruapehu and Ngauruhoe. The third one is known to *Lord of the Rings* movie fans as Mount Doom. Outdoor enthusiasts often break their journey at the national park, a convenient halfway stop on the trip, for the chance to walk the Tongariro Crossing, a tough 19km hike.

When we did this trek in December 2012, we were astounded at how ill-prepared our fellow walkers were. Before social media influencers replaced guidebook writers, the trip was featured by the likes of Lonely Planet and the Rough Guides. It was sold to international tourists as one of the world's greatest one-day hikes, so many assumed they could do it in trainers. We were warned by fellow New

Zealanders that walking boots, hiking poles, plenty of water and snacks were essential, as there is nothing but landscape on this epic journey.

Even though the walk starts at 1,120m above sea level, the first section is a climb from a valley to the saddle between Mount Tongariro and Mount Ngauruhoe. Then you pass through South Crater before climbing again to Red Crater, which at 1,886m is the highest point on the crossing.

As we were walking in peak tourist season, our party of four encountered a steady stream of fellow walkers along the way. Where the path was narrow, we had to climb up rocks in single file, stuck behind a group of Californian college students from Stanford, who were so engrossed in heated discussions about their internet start-ups that they didn't once lift their heads to be in the moment, treating the trip like a tick-box exercise.

Then there was the unfortunate man from South Korea. He spoke no English, but despite this, using much gesticulating, other walkers counselled him not to risk the hike in boat shoes. He ignored the advice, and as the day wore on, his shoes began to shred. By the time we started to descend, he had plastic bags tied around both his shoes to try to protect his feet from the sharp rocks. I couldn't bring myself to watch as he slid down the rock scree track that I was about to descend.

Even though I had been warned that this descent was the steepest part of the track, it hadn't occurred to me, until I looked down at the ground, that the scree rocks would mean an uncontrolled slide at every step. And worst of all, there was neither a rope nor any vegetation between me and the Emerald Lakes, 1,886 metres below. But as I was figuring out how I was going to get down, I heard a young woman a few steps behind me calling out.

'I can't do it, I'm turning back,' she said.

This gave me something new to focus on. I turned around to face her.

'We'll do it together,' I said, hoping she couldn't hear the fear in my voice. 'One step at a time. Give me your hand.' I kept telling myself that if I was scared, she was ten times worse.

'I'll turn back,' she said.

'It's too far. We're three quarters of the way now. We've just got to get through this bit, then we're nearly there.' Again, I reached for her hand. 'We can do it.' And zigzagging down the slope, sliding one foot then the other, we did exactly that and got down in one piece.

Once we were in the valley, the track was mostly flat, although we were sent on a detour for an extra kilometre to avoid the hazardous volcanic fissures on the path. If we'd stepped in one by mistake, it would have taken our feet off. Eleven years on, I marvel that I survived this once-in-a-lifetime adventure, but at the same time, I'm glad to be revisiting it. From the comfort of our train, that is.

We arrive at Wellington railway station 11-and-a-half hours after we set off, having covered 681km (423 miles). We jump into a cab and are driven to our Airbnb. I offload our luggage while BB Lookalike pays the taxi driver, who has sneakily turned his meter off and charges him double the price the journey should have cost. I call the cab company, telling the operator the time and date of our pickup. They promise to investigate it, but never do.

Of all the places to be ripped off, I never thought it would be in good old New Zealand. But I don't let it spoil my holiday.

9

We're All Going on a Bear Hunt

In 2023, BB Lookalike is awarded extended study leave and decides to split it between Australia and the UK. For the first time since we moved, he has time to spend with family and friends in England, even celebrating his milestone birthday with them.

We return to Australia via Vancouver, Canada, where BB Lookalike will be running a university seminar for the research component of his study leave. I've yet to visit Vancouver, but everyone I know who's been raves about it. My first visit to Canada was in the depths of winter and left a lasting impression—mostly bad. We scored free flight tickets to New York one freezing January, thanks to a daft promotion by a vacuum cleaner company, then took an Amtrak train to Montreal where it was minus 26 Celsius. I spent the whole time indoors, and when I looked out the window and saw a poster outside a travel agent's advertising holidays in the summer weather of New Zealand, I burst into tears.

Luckily, this time we are visiting in early autumn, not the depths of the Northern Hemisphere winter. On 23

September 2023, as we wait for our afternoon Air Canada flight at Heathrow, I get chatting to a fellow passenger. She kindly offers me the paperback she's just finished reading. I take a glance at the title—a gory horror. Not my thing at all.

'I'd love to read that,' I lie. 'But I have plenty of books on this,' I say, as I proffer my Kindle.

'I've never tried reading with one of those,' she tells me.

'I prefer a real book too, but this is really useful when I'm travelling.'

'And what brings you folks to British Columbia?' she asks.

'I'll be sightseeing while my husband is working,' I reply. 'But after the teaching finishes, we're going over to Vancouver Island on a bear spotting tour.'

'Bears! I have them in my back yard, you should come and visit me.'

'We would if we had time,' I say, as something tells me her offer is genuine.

While we line up, forming an orderly queue at the departure gate (no gate lice here!), I overhear a conversation about tipping. It's not something I've given a moment's thought to before. We only ever tip in Australia when the service in a restaurant is good, or in a taxi if the driver has found a shortcut. There's no blanket tipping like in the USA, where you are effectively subsidising employers who neglect to pay their staff a decent minimum wage. Australia pays its workers (in 2023) a generous minimum of $24.10 per hour. Naively, I assumed that Canada would be like Australia, and as the minimum wage at the time of writing is $17.30 per hour, it's a darn sight better than its southern neighbour. But despite this, its tipping culture emulates the USA. I will need to get my head around tipping everyone 20 per cent.

As we settle down in our seats and buckle up, a female voice on the intercom greets us and tells us that she is Captain Susan.

Way to go, Air Canada!

I sneak a furtive glance at the men sitting along the row from us. Not one flinches. Canadians must be cool with female pilots then. It's been a while since I've listened to an authoritative female voice issuing instructions from the flight deck, and when I have, she's usually been the co-pilot. And if I recall, the last time I flew with a female pilot, I spotted a distinct shift in the seat from the older man sitting next to me. All I could think about then was that there'd been a female commander on the Space Shuttle, a lady boss of the International Space Station and, of course, Ellen Ripley, who should receive an honourable mention even though it took until *Alien 3* for her to rise to the rank of Lieutenant.

I'm even more impressed with the airline when we arrive at the airbridge at Vancouver and an announcement rings out as we are about to disembark.

'Folks, I'm Brian Jones, head of pilot training, and I have had the pleasure of promoting Captain Susan to the rank she now holds. A First Officer for 20 years, she passed her final tests on our flight.'

We duly clap and as we disembark, Captain Susan greets us at the aircraft door. I want to tell her that she's an inspiration to all young women who aspire to learn to fly, but that sounds cringy.

'Congratulations,' I say lamely, as she pumps my hand.

Street of the Living Dead

After our ten-hour flight, we jump in a cab and head off Downtown. We will be staying for four nights at the three-star Granville Suites at 718 Drake Street, which is charging $976CA—$1,089AU or £545—for two nights. I've heard rumours that Vancouver hotel prices are exorbitant, but this is outrageous. Even in London, you could get a four-star hotel for that price.

I find out later that the hotel is surge pricing because of demand as the Coldplay tour is here this weekend. It's just as well that two out of our four nights are being subsidised by work.

Despite these prices, we're at the grungy, studenty end of town. When we go out for an early dinner at a local Mexican taqueria, we watch zombies wander trance-like all over the pavement.

'I reckon it must be fentanyl,' I say. 'They're like the living dead. And there's me thinking I've seen everything there is to see on Fitzroy St in Kilda.' In Melbourne, addicts take ice (crystal meth) and heroin, which are dangerous enough, but fentanyl, the synthetic opioid, is in a different league. A small amount would be enough to kill you in minutes as it's 50 to 100 times more potent than morphine, the heroin derivative.

The next day, after an early morning walk where we avoid the main street in case we come across more of the living dead, we poke our heads around the door of the hotel bar/restaurant to see what the breakfast offerings are.

'It all looks a bit beige, like their decor,' I say. 'I'm sure we could do better at a neighbourhood joint. Let's try a block over towards Stanley Park. I can't face Drake Street in the cold light of day.'

It's amazing the difference just one block makes. We find a cafe with tempting breakfast dishes. I have the Scandinavian option of wild salmon, avocado and a poached egg. It's delicious.

The next evening, we walk in the other direction, across the Granville Street Bridge towards Granville Island, with its seafood restaurants and buzzy atmosphere. However, as we walk along the boardwalk by the harbour, hundreds of little mice dart out from under the planks. I've never seen so many.

At least they aren't rats.

At the seafood restaurant, I do a quick scan of the floor before walking in. No mice to be seen. We are shown to one of the outdoor tables on the terrace, all of which have heating, which is a relief as even though it is still only late September, it's much cooler at night than I expected.

I order fish and chips, Vancouver style, choosing halibut, which is a premium fish in the UK. The chips are twice-cooked and perfect—crunchy on the outside and soft in the middle, just the way I like them. The plate comes with a wedge of lemon and coleslaw. As I'm a chips and mayonnaise fan, the coleslaw gives me the mayonnaise hit combined with a virtual-signalling combo of raw carrot, a smattering of red onion and cabbage.

On Monday night, I brave Drake Street alone to get to Granville Street. I walk in the direction of the cruise ship terminal to meet BB Lookalike as his colleagues have invited us out for a meal after work. Once I hit Downtown, near the art gallery and law courts, the street morphs into a desirable gentrified neighbourhood. It's raining, which is something I'd have to get used to if I lived here as it rains a lot. Even more than in England, which is saying something.

We rendezvous at 6pm and eat at a nearby Italian restaurant in a cosy basement. The atmosphere is jovial rather than stuffy, which I'm relieved about. Some post-work dinners I've gone to, people have only wanted to talk shop. But not tonight. BB Lookalike's departmental colleagues tell us how far out of town they have to live to be able to afford to rent or buy a place. That sounds like nearly every city in the developed world, where only the highest earners can afford to live centrally.

'What's it like here in the winter?' I ask.

'Treacherous up where I live in the hills, especially when it's icy,' a woman tells me. 'I can practically skate all the way down to the train station.'

'That's not a problem we have in downtown Melbourne, although it can get icy in the hills, like here,' I say. We are out of there by 8.30pm. Despite it not being skating weather just yet, we're mindful that these folks have still to travel some distance home when we are but a 20-minute stroll away from our hotel.

Bears Galore!

The next morning we're up bright and early to catch the 08.45 ferry from Horseshoe Bay to Vancouver Island, where our Bear Tour is to take place. The terminal is some way out of town and it takes 45 minutes in a taxi to get there. The ferry is packed with school kids with backpacks and hiking gear, looking like they're heading off to a wilderness camp.

The trip across the Strait of Georgia, which is between the British Columbia mainland and Vancouver Island, takes one hour and 45 minutes. We get chatting to a lady with family in the USA and she tells us that they have an exit strategy. If Donald Trump were to win the 2024 election, they'll all return to Canada.

At the little town of Nanaimo, we have a fifteen-minute

wait for our bus up to Campbell River. When I say bus, it's a minibus and there are only eight of us onboard. The driver is friendly and matter of fact, and before we can say, "Smarter than the average bear", we're off on our bear hunt.

We pass several little towns that gradually get smaller and smaller as we make our way up the island, moving out of the built-up area, the houses becoming more scattered. But there's still a steady stream of logging and construction trucks that pass us along the highway. I was expecting the island to be more of a wilderness. But evidently Campbell River is a thriving regional town.

Vancouver Island is one-and-a-half times the size of Wales and we are seeing a fraction of it. As is so often the case with our travels, we grab a few days either side of BB Lookalike's work trips to fit in as much as we can in the limited time we have.

Because I failed to research how big the town we're staying in is and how much traffic passes through, as soon as I see our self-catering motel beside Island Highway, I regret my choice. The sitting room, kitchen and deck look out onto the tranquil waters towards Quadra Island. But the bedroom is at the front, right near the highway. I keep my fingers crossed for a night curfew of noisy vehicles and their air brakes, but sadly there's a steady stream ploughing up and down the highway. I have such a disturbed night, I end up sleeping on the sofa bed in the living room.

The next morning, I forget about my bad night's sleep. Today is the day of our excursion, the reason we came here, and I can't wait. We're out the door at 7am as our call time for the Great Bears of Bute boat trip is 7.30. I'm keeping all fingers and toes crossed that I've chosen the right tour. It was a toss-up between basing ourselves in the laid-back surfing town of Tofino to see black bears or here in Campbell River to see grizzlies. If I only ever get to hang out with bears in the wild once, it has to be the big, scary ones.

Both tours involve boat travel as there are no bear habitats on the island. The grizzlies tour crosses inland waterways, which can, of course, be choppy if the weather is bad, but that's nothing compared with the open sea. The added attraction is that our bear trip is run by an indigenous tour group, the Homalco First Nation, who have a long history of stewardship of their lands. They are known as "the people of the fast-running waters", named after the turbulent waters surrounding Bute Inlet. Their connection to the land goes so far back in time that there is no record or memory of when they established their community here.

For two people, the cost is $1,170 CA or £650 for a full day's trip. A percentage goes towards salmon and bear conservation, which we are happy to support. And as this is our only excursion while we are here, we want to spend our money on a unique wildlife experience with guides who are passionate about the place they call home.

Although the tour runs from Vancouver Island, our destination is Orford Bay on the mainland of British Columbia. The boat is a comfortable-looking craft with seating out the front on deck, and inside is a cosy cabin. It's designed to take no more than 12 passengers. The Homalco First Nation come across as a highly professional outfit and I feel very reassured.

As we wait to board the boat, we make small talk with an older couple from England. The lady is a Chatty Cathy and doesn't stop talking as we glide across the bay.

'Let's sit outside,' I whisper to BB Lookalike after a while of getting my ear bent. 'We can always come back in if it's too cold.' We leave the bore inside with her husband

and grab a seat at the front of the boat. There's barely a breath of wind and the sea is as smooth and glossy as paint. It starts to drizzle, but that doesn't detract from the beauty of the scenery—clear waters the colour of a forest, surrounded by pointy hills and mountains. The captain cuts the engine and we drift silently along as we pass a colony of sea lions up on the rocks. They remind me of dogs on a group outing in Albert Park, with their excited barks and whines.

After two hours we arrive at the mouth of Bute Inlet and make our way up to Orford Bay. As we get ready to disembark, we are briefed because we are now in bear country. I'm so excited I can't do anything but look around with childlike glee, scanning the horizon for bears.

As we step off the boat at the jetty at Orford Bay, our guides James and Chyanne greet us and escort us to a waiting minibus. We make the short trip to their base and are welcomed with a brief introduction about the culture and history of the Homalco. It reminds me of a "Welcome to Country" ceremony in Australia.

After drinks and snacks, we get back on the bus and are driven around various locations along the Orford River. The bears come here to gorge on Pacific salmon before they hibernate for the winter. I find out later that it was only because of a far-reaching decision taken by the Homalco forty years ago that the bears are here at all. In the 1980s, they developed a salmon hatchery at Orford Bay. And when the bears started coming, they opened the area for tourism.

We're very fortunate that we've timed our visit in peak Pacific salmon running season. Chyanne drives for ten minutes, bumping along the river, and then pulls up at our first stop, where James has spotted a huge bear standing in the middle of the river.

'Look, cubs.'

We stare, transfixed. I can scarcely take my eyes off the female, who's slapping her paws on the water and piercing an enormous Pacific salmon in her claws, before shovelling it into her mouth. And then I spot her two cubs, standing timidly at the water's edge, watching their mother, but not yet ready to join in.

We get off the bus and stand behind it. Chatty Cathy starts up again, but James escorts her around to the side of the bus, away from the rest of us, and manages to persuade her to shut up. We are but 20 to 30 metres away from the bears, but luckily the roar of the flowing river drowns out even Chatty Cathy. The big female, who could kill any one of us with one swipe of her razor-sharp claws, is in a food coma and stares down into the water as the running buffet of chum glides past her.

'She can't smell us from the middle of the water,' James says. As we snap away, taking photos, his words lull us into a false sense of security. Suddenly, there's a rustling sound behind us. I glance around. Lumbering towards the family group is another bear, a large adolescent male from a previous litter who has come to join in the feeding frenzy. He sees the plentiful supply of fish and walks in the opposite direction, away from the three bears, stepping out into the middle of the river.

James tells us if it was earlier in the season and the bears were competing for fish, the female would have attacked the interloper to protect her cubs, but now there's enough food to go around. However, her cubs are nervous and retreat, well away from the young male. He eats a few fish and then, just as quickly as he arrived, he scampers up the bank, heading straight towards our tour bus. All of us make it safely on board before he lumbers past into the forest. In fact, I've never got back on a bus so fast!

I sit in my seat, heart pounding. Our bear count so far is four. Never in my wildest dreams did I think we'd get this lucky.

Chyanne drives off down river towards several hides, which we climb into. This time, there are no bears. Our last destination is like the first and we see two lone bears, both males, fishing in the middle of the river, a respectable distance from each other. But I'm still buzzing from the encounter with the mother and her two cubs, and that's the memory I take with me as we return to the boat and head back towards Campbell River.

The Deadly Sniffles

Our time on Vancouver Island is all too brief and the next morning, we are first to board the minibus to Nanaimo to meet the ferry back to the mainland. At our second stop, a young couple—late teens or early twenties—get on. They are dressed as goths, with ripped clothes, dyed-black hair and skull-and-crossbones rings. They choose the seats directly behind us, the young woman sitting behind me and the young man behind BB Lookalike.

Being in a confined space with strangers, I have taken the precaution of masking up. In the three years since the start of the Covid 19 pandemic, we have both avoided catching it. I've worn masks on planes and in airports, and we are two of the last members of the extended family not to have succumbed.

And it's then that we hear sniffing from right behind us. I peer around; it's the young goth seated directly behind BB Lookalike, who is directing all the spray coming out of his nose over him. I freeze up, willing the nasal assault to bypass me.

'Shall we move seats?' I ask BB Lookalike. He shakes his head as we approach the next stop where a line of passengers waits to board.

'No point,' he says, indicating the queue. Sure enough, once these travellers board, the minibus is at full capacity.

Apart from the young couple and us, the rest are solitary travellers, who keep to themselves. For the next two hours, I look out the window, trying to concentrate on the scenery, but cringing inwardly every time there's nasal action from behind us. Once we arrive at Nanaimo, we wait for the ferry outdoors, breathing in the sea air after the stale conditions on the bus.

On arrival in Vancouver, we spend our last night in a serviced apartment near English Bay, a vibrant neighbourhood with seaside walks, bars and cafés. After a leisurely breakfast the next morning, we check out at ten. We arrange with the concierge to leave our suitcases in a locker and promise to collect them by late afternoon, then spend the day walking along the 10km Stanley Park Seawall loop. The path is shared with cyclists who must travel anticlockwise or, as they'd say in Canada, counterclockwise. This means we can see the cyclists as we walk towards them, and more importantly, they can see us.

After our epic walk, we return to the apartment to grab our bags. Our taxi crawls for most of the way to the airport as it's Friday night and every man, woman and dog appears to be heading away for the weekend. Our taxi driver, who is of Indian heritage but hails from Fiji, suggests that next time we should travel on Fiji Airways, as that way we'd get to stop over in Fiji on our way to New Zealand. Not that he's biased.

'I'd never want to leave,' I say.

At check-in, the very helpful Air New Zealand representative notes we aren't seated together and, before I can stop her, moves me next to BB Lookalike. I don't look too closely at where I've been assigned, hoping it will be a better seat. But to my horror, for the next 14 hours, we will sit in the middle two seats on the last row, nearest the bathrooms. The cabin crew take pity on us and bring us extra drinks, stop to chat—anything to alleviate our plight in the worst seats in the house. They are also meticulous about cleaning the bathrooms regularly, so what we thought was going to be the trip from hell turns out to be a pleasant flight.

Arriving in Auckland, we are picked up by our host and pass a brilliant day in the company of friends, before an early start the next day to catch our three-hour flight back to Melbourne. The morning after our arrival home, BB Lookalike complains of feeling under the weather with a runny nose and sore throat. As a precaution he takes a Covid test.

He tests positive.

The first thing I do is message all the friends we mixed with in New Zealand to apologise and suggest they get tested. It's a huge relief that they all test negative. All the vaccinations and boosters BB Lookalike has had mitigate the severity of the illness and after a week, he is no longer infectious. I, meanwhile, have been masking up (not quite wearing full PPE), as well as flinging open all the windows and doors and camping out at the opposite end of the apartment to him. I've prepared meals and then left them outside BB Lookalike's bedroom on a tray, just like he's in prison or hotel quarantine. You may regard this as overkill, but I'm not yet ready to relinquish my status as one of the last ones in the extended family to be Covid free.

All that changes in early 2025 when I catch it off a healthcare professional who is sniffing while she's treating me. I put it down to "just a cold" and end up with the

Omicron variant, the one that comes with a burning sore throat. It's so painful that I can barely swallow. I call the GP in desperation. He prescribes me very strong painkillers, which knock me out for three days. However, when I wake up, I'm no longer in agony.

The last Covid-free one standing in the family holds that record to this day.

10

Christmas in the South Island

After the embarrassment of taking Covid to Auckland in October, we return to New Zealand as tourists for Christmas 2023. BB Lookalike has never been to Queenstown, despite living in New Zealand for five years. There's a direct flight from Melbourne and what's more, it's quicker to get to than many places in Australia.

The flight across the Tasman on 22 December is uneventful—calm, even—until we reach the coastline of Fiordland. As the plane descends, we fly through green valleys, surrounded by vertiginous mountains. The plane flies so close to the jagged peaks, I involuntarily breathe in. There's a light breeze blowing and little in the way of wind shear, so we get off lightly. But I wouldn't fancy doing this in bad weather.

Tourists flock here for the spectacular mountain and lake scenery, and if there's a white-knuckle ride thrown in with the cost of an airfare, bring it on. On every adrenalin junkie's bucket list, Queenstown is the place where being dangled by the feet from a rope over the fast-flowing Shotover river was invented. That's torture to me, but others pay good money to go bungee jumping. The only adrenalin-fuelled sport I'll be doing is driving around the Southern Lakes' twisty roads.

After we land safely, I text our hire car company. The Very Cheap Cars representative pick us up and takes us to their base, behind the airport. The cost of the rental for ten days is $940NZ, which beats the competition by a third. But, of course, the pay-off is that the car is at least five years old, with lots of dents and low tech. As I'm the sort who would lock themselves out of their car by mistake, I'm happy with a key for the ignition, rather than a fancy keyless model. I do cringe at the Very Cheap Cars bumper sticker, praying I don't run into anyone I know.

Once the visual inspection is over and I'm satisfied that the windscreen wipers and the indicators operate like they do in all the other cars I've ever driven, it's time to set the GPS to our apartment, Alpine Village Views, 643 Frankton Road.

I edge my way gingerly out of the parking lot of Very Cheap Cars and join the stream of traffic leaving the airport. I choose the left-hand lane, to turn onto the main road between the airport and the town centre. All the other drivers, even those who are clearly tourists and unused to driving on the left-hand side of the road, give me a wide berth.

Of course, that's the bumper sticker talking.

It's as good as wearing a baseball cap that says Dumb Tourist Alert—Avoid at All Costs. I grew up here and although I might not know the lower South Island, I have more experience driving on New Zealand roads than this lot put together.

The apartment complex is in Frankton, near the airport and at the budget end of Queenstown, but it's still costing us $2,500NZ for the ten-day booking. In this town, you'd be lucky to get anything for less than that, especially a spacious one-bedroom apartment with a balcony overlooking Lake Wakitipu and the mountains.

Queenstown isn't like the rest of New Zealand. Think of it like Aspen, Colorado, attracting well-heeled visitors who ski by day, then hit the bars at night. And in the summer, the international visitors come for the wine tourism, as well as the magnificent scenery.

The Haves and the Have Nots

As we aren't travelling with any family and friends, we are keen to find a different way of marking Christmas Day. I'm on the waiting list for a cancellation at Nest, the fine-dining restaurant at Kamana Lakehouse, a luxury lodge, which charges from $730NZ a night for a double room during the festive period. The restaurant is offering a nine-course tasting menu on Christmas Day which, with the matching wines, will cost $400NZ per person. With neither presents nor a large crowd to cater for, we have agreed that, for an unforgettable one-off celebration, this will do very nicely.

We are lucky. Over the next couple of days, the wished-for cancellation comes in and our booking is secured. Our dining slot is 7pm and we catch an Uber to the restaurant so we can both enjoy the wines.

I thank the driver who picks us up for working on Christmas Day.

'It's not a festival I celebrate, so I'm happy to work,' he says.

'How do you like Queenstown and what drew you here?' I ask.

'The skiing,' he tells me. 'I come from Nepal, so I feel very at home in the mountains.'

'And in the summer?'

'I hike.'

My curiosity gets the better of me. 'How long have you been here, if you don't mind me asking?'

'Nine years.'

'You must like it. But the cost of accommodation is so high, that must be a challenge?'

'That's the worst part of living here. I can't afford to stay in Queenstown. I live in a caravan in Glenorchy, along with many others who work here.'

Nine years, living in a cramped caravan! Why aren't the employers providing their staff with somewhere decent to live?

'That must be so cold in the winter.

'It reminds me of Nepal,' he says. 'But at least here I have a car, even if I have to chip the ice off it in the mornings.'

Glenorchy is 46km and a 45 minute to an hour drive from Queenstown along a treacherous road with hairpin bends. Even in perfect conditions, you have to have your wits about you. I'm relieved to hear from our driver that the road is gritted in winter.

'Would you ever think of moving to Australia? At least you'd be able to have a roof over your head,' I say.

'Many of my friends have moved there. But it is just the beach, isn't it? And I love mountains,' he replies.

As soon as we arrive at the entrance to Kamana Lake-house, we get out of the car and I turn to pay our driver.

'I wish you all the best, wherever you end up,' I say.

'Thanks for the chat,' he replies. He's certainly put me straight about what sort of conditions he and his fellow workers have to put up with. I can only hope that his life gets easier.

Perched on the top of a hill overlooking Lake Wakitipu, the hotel is a combination of triple-glazed glass and expensive schist stone. I don't think I've ever been anywhere else this fancy in New Zealand. As we walk into the bar area of the restaurant, there before us is Lake Wakitipu sparkling in the sunshine.

Once we've taken in the view, a waiter comes over to us, ushers us to a bar table and brings over glasses of champagne. The first thing that strikes me is the conversation going on around me. People are speaking in French, German, or American English, but not one, including the front-of-house staff, appears to be a New Zealander. We could be in an exclusive mountain resort anywhere in the world, except, of course, for the vista of the Remarkables and Lake Wakitipu. The Queenstown of 40 years ago, when I last visited, was a ski town for New Zealanders. Today it's the playground for the global elite.

The contrast between the haves and the have nots couldn't be starker. The have nots are the invisible workers, like our Uber driver and the staff at the restaurant, who help run this town. The haves are people like us who can afford to eat here. But as it's Christmas Day and we're here to celebrate, I set those thoughts aside and immerse myself in the moment as we are ushered to our table and presented with the tasting menu and the wine pairings.

As soon as we sit down, a waiter arrives with the pre-dinner hors d'oeuvre, which is Fermented Potato Bread with whipped chive creme fraiche. I take a bite of the bread, which is still warm. It works perfectly with the rest of my champagne.

There's a festive atmosphere at table. A family group, speaking French, with children aged between about seven and seventeen, sit down and eat their way through the menu like they're seasoned pros. Being French, a nationality renowned for culinary expertise, they probably are.

All the children have perfect table manners, and not one of them questions what's put in front of them.

Next to us, a young American couple ask us apologetically if we can take their photograph on the terrace. They're on their honeymoon, they tell us.

'Oh, where from?' I ask.

'Texas,' the husband says, then adds quickly, 'Austin, Texas.' Although I've never been to Texas, apart from the airport at Houston, I know enough about Austin. Instead of the oil barons and Stetsons synonymous with the state, it's a liberal student town with a very good arts university.

I beam at him. 'Austin has a famous writers' programme, doesn't it?' I ask.

'Yes,' he says. 'The Michener Centre at The University of Texas.' As I sit down after the "photo shoot", the sommelier comes over with our second wine match, while a waiter places our first seafood course in front of us: Blackfoot paua, barbecued on skewers, with a seaweed glaze. Paua is the Maori name for abalone, a species of edible sea snail and a delicacy in many Asian countries. The paua is beautifully presented on its iridescent shell, shimmering in shades of teal and ocean blue. The smoky flavour and just-cooked texture are a winner.

It's followed by scampi ceviche, served raw, accompanied by avocado sorbet and chilli with pickled shallots. The artful arrangement on the plate is indicative of one of the kitchen brigade plating in a particular way. I wouldn't be surprised if they arranged those shallots with tweezers.

This is followed by a cold soup, or rather, a summer courgette blossom with wild pork and fermented tomato gazpacho. I have first-hand experience of the wild porkers that run around in the New Zealand bush; I had a run-in with one once in the shape of an angry wild boar, complete with tusks, who came charging across my path when I was 13 and out horse-riding on my own. It was all too much for my sweet horse, who, like most equines, hated the smell of pigs. She dumped me on the track, a couple of miles from home, then promptly bolted, while I limped home on foot.

Then a palate-cleansing break in the form of a lemon sorbet prepares us for the two highlights of the menu. The first is Fiordland crayfish tortellini served in a miso bisque with charred sweetcorn. The bisque is clear, with a silken texture, and each of the three tortellini is the size of a fingernail.

The last main course is about the nearest the menu gets to anything vaguely Christmassy: Duck served two ways with a spiced plum puree on the side. We sip the last of our matching wines, a Pinot Noir from a boutique vineyard. Like all the other wine pairings we've had here, it's delicious.

There is a dessert wine to follow, which BB Lookalike has. I taste it, but I'm too busy marvelling at the pudding—a local cherry and vanilla parfait with elderflower—to have a full glass. Central Otago cherries are prized throughout the country and we look out for them every Christmas when we're in New Zealand. And for the grand finale it's the cheese course—goat curd, burnt honey with celery salt, served with Lavosh biscuits and figs from Marlborough.

How we get through all this, I'll never know. And it's not like I can put my feet up on Boxing Day as we have a big trip ahead of us.

Back on the Road

The next day, we head off on a two-day excursion to Milford Sound via Te Anau. Milford Sound is, in fact, a fiord, carved out of glaciers in a setting framed by spectacular mountains. It is on every tourist itinerary, so we are bracing ourselves for coaches and crowds.

We leave late morning on Boxing Day, taking our time. We could have driven the whole way in one hit, but we're here for a holiday, not a tick-box exercise. The route takes us alongside Lake Wakatipu, where I obediently obey every single sign for the recommended speed limit on each bend. I'm not taking any chances with my hire car.

It takes just over two-and-a-half hours to drive the 171km to Te Anau, a busy little town at this time of the year. It's too early to check into our hotel, the modern but characterless Distinction Luxmore, which is, we discover, a favourite of tour groups. But as breakfast is thrown in and the room looks comfortable, it suits us fine.

While we're waiting to check in, our first stop is the pie shop, and it's not just any old pie shop either. Miles Better Pies is the home of gourmet bakes, and for me it's a toss-up between local venison and plum sauce or seafood. I choose the venison pie as we did have a lot of seafood last night. The pastry is crisp and the generous filling makes it difficult to eat without a knife and fork. I get through at least six serviettes, but it's a fantastic lunch. I didn't think I'd be able to eat another thing after our blow-out yesterday.

Once we've had our pie, we head out for a walk alongside Lake Te Anau. Along the way, we pass the jetty for the boat pick-up to take walkers for a day's outing on the Kepler Track. I wish I'd added this on to our itinerary, but I'll save it for our next visit.

I potter around the tourist information office and get chatting to one of the volunteers.

'Te Anau seems more like a real place, where local people live,' I remark. 'Unlike Queenstown.'

'It's a nightmare, Queenstown,' she replies. 'One of our kids plays sport there and sometimes we have to stay over. We can't afford even the most basic accommodation, so we take our caravan and stay in the caravan park.'

I tell her about the living conditions of the Uber driver who took us to the restaurant yesterday.

'Soon there won't be any staff left, willing to put up with living conditions like that,' the volunteer says, 'and the fancy places will have to start building affordable accommodation. But I don't see that happening anytime soon.'

'You're right. On our next visit, I think we'll give Queenstown a swerve and come straight here instead.'

'You'd be very welcome,' she says. And then I remember why I came into the tourist office in the first place and ask advice about where to go for dinner.

'There's not much open as it's Boxing Day. Try Pizzeria Paradiso, but that'll be heaving, so go early.'

'Thanks for the tip,' I say as we walk out towards the hotel, which is barely 20 metres away, to check in.

Early evening, we take the volunteer's advice and get the last table at the pizzeria before the hordes arrive. It doesn't matter how long it takes to get served, we're lucky we found this place. And the atmosphere is lively.

After a sound sleep in a comfortable bed, we make our way to breakfast at 7.30am and hit peak tour group time. The wait staff are apologetic, but I feel sorry for them as they run around, madly clearing tables so that we can sit down.

Refreshed after our stay, I'm ready for today's drive. The road to Milford Sound is billed as one of New Zealand's greatest driving routes. But there are many hazards to watch out for along the way.

As we set off, I'm impressed there's a recommended maximum speed on every bend in the twisty road. I obey each one. It's perfect driving conditions: a beautifully clear day with bright sunshine and a cobalt blue sky. The problem, though, is all the other tourists. They drive so erratically, we conclude they must never before have travelled on a single carriageway with very limited passing places.

Driving into Milford Sound "Village," after overshooting the free carpark on the outskirts of "town," I join the long line of packed cars and campervans full of tourists, all wanting to experience a boat trip on the fiord. I swing into the second carpark, closer to the boat ramp and look in vain for a free space.

Nothing.

I try the third carpark but all that's left is scarcely room to park a Harley Davidson. And then it dawns on me. There's only one way in and out of Milford Sound and if I don't find somewhere to park, we'll be on our way back to Queenstown, having to 'fess up that we missed out on New Zealand's greatest natural wonder. And if you're wondering why we couldn't simply abandon the car on the side of the road and walk, the skinny road out is a series of hairpin bends, sandwiched between pointy rocks on both sides.

We could try our luck at the free parking on the outskirts, but if the number of vehicles clogging the road is anything to go by, everyone else has already tried there. I turn around, head out of the carpark towards the Visitors' Centre—in front of which are, wait for it—no cars. I scan for No Parking signs, pull in and park up right outside. No sooner do I get out of the car and grab a parking ticket out of the nearest machine, than I watch every other driver behind me, desperately trying to angle park in a space the size of a horse box. Luckily, I'm at the front so no one (in theory) can box me in.

Phew! That was a close one.

We grab a coffee at the Visitors' Centre, which is an informal office for all the helicopter pilots who fly well-heeled tourists on private trips to view Milford Sound from the air. We, though, are going on a Nature Discovery Cruise, which is booked for 12.15pm. But before we set off, we cover ourselves with tropical strength bug spray. Because the one thing that no one tells you about New Zealand's greatest tourist attraction is that in the summer, the sandflies will bite you on every bit of exposed skin, unless you're covered head to toe. Sandflies are smaller and meaner than mosquitos, so you'll feel their sharp sting, but won't have seen them coming. As we queue for the cruise, we overhear a family from overseas with two young children, who are evidently under attack from the pesky bugs.

'Mummy, help, make them stop,' one child cries.

'Can we sit inside?' the other pleads. We offer our sympathies along with our bug spray.

Our cruise is a two hour tour, which costs just shy of $300 NZ or $263 AUD for two. And the weather conditions are perfect, which is a miracle, as there are 182 rain days at Milford Sound per year and high summer is the wettest time of the year. And when I say rain, I mean, seven metres a year, making Fiordland one of the wettest places on earth.

The ship glides through glossy, blue black waters and our vessel is but an insignificant dot between the towering glacial peaks of Fiordland National Park, one of New Zealand's last remaining wilderness areas. We pass cascading waterfalls and in the distance glimpse snow covered peaks.

As there is barely any wind, the captain takes our ship a little further today than the regular cruise, all the way to the Tasman Sea. I can hardly contain myself as, at last, I can say that I have finally been to the West Coast of the

South Island. I may have grown up in New Zealand's South Island, but I only had to look at a hairpin bend before I felt sick and my parents had to abandon their plans to take our family on road trips that involved steep, twisty roads.

On one of the few long, straight stretches on the drive back to Queenstown, we observe a family of tourists by the side of the road, near a flock of keas. Native to New Zealand, keas are the world's only mountain parrot. Their olive-green colour blends in brilliantly with the alpine environment, until you spot the bright orange under the wings. Keas have an impressively large curved beak, which they use as a tool, like a handy tin opener. They're highly intelligent and sociable, so unsuspecting tourists like to interact with them.

Keas regard humans as easy to outwit. As well as their beaks, these parrots use their claws as tools, and have been known to break into huts or steal a hiker's lunch out of their backpack. And if you leave a car in a mountain carpark overnight, you could well come back to a broken aerial, or the windscreen wipers shredded.

This family of tourists is going to be finding out about kea-induced mayhem the hard way.

Horse Riding in the Misty Mountains

We don't spot any keas in Glenorchy, the small town at the top of Lake Wakitipu. We're there for the chance to go horse riding with a trekking company specialising in Parelli Natural Horsemanship, where the horses are ridden in bitless bridles. Where I ride in England, horses new to the school are put through their paces using Parelli training. The opposite of the fear-based training and force that is still too common in the equestrian world, it aims to bring the best out of horse and rider using communication, psychology and knowledge of horses' instincts.

As BB Lookalike has only ever been on a horse once before in his life, I book an hour-and-a-half walk-only ride. The treks take place in the Dart Valley with a stunning backdrop of pointy mountains, which for movie buffs was the setting for Isengard in the *Lord of the Rings* films, where Gandalf rides to meet Saruman. Not only that, but Glenorchy stood in for the Misty Mountains in *The Hobbit*. I can't think of anywhere I'd rather ride on holiday than here. I don't think there is anywhere more beautiful.

When we arrive for the trek, we are assigned horses depending on our experience, height and weight. I stupidly volunteer that I'm an experienced rider.

My training consists of English style riding, mostly dressage and hacking out. Up until the age of 17, I rode in cross country and show jumping competitions. At this trekking company, we ride in a Western saddle, which is comfortable and secure. As this is Parelli, the horses are steered with cues. As a child, I would sometimes ride my pony without a saddle, but riding without a bit in the horse's mouth is a first for me. It's something I will have to get used to.

My first challenge is to get on the horse. In English style riding, you step up onto a mounting block on the left-hand side of the horse, put your left foot into the stirrup and fling your right leg over the horse, who is held by a groom. At this riding school, we are instructed to get on from the right-hand side. It's done for safety reasons, as being able to get on from either side gives you more options in challenging terrain. But it's a strange sensation.

Once I'm in the Western saddle, it feels like I'm sitting in a chair, rather than on a horse.

What would happen if I needed to get out of it in a hurry?

In English style riding, you dismount by taking both feet out of the stirrups, swinging your right leg over the horse's back, then sliding down to the ground as softly as possible. We are taught that in Western riding, you must keep your left foot in the stirrup. This is counter-intuitive because if your horse is spooked and bolts, you could be dragged along.

It's not going to happen today, I tell myself. Once our "getting to know our horse" session is over, we ride out in a group of seven riders and two instructors. Our first adventure is to cross the Dart River. It's a trip these horses do most days and they are very sure-footed, or should that be sure-hoofed?

My horse is confident as he follows the herd into and across the river. It is wide and mostly shallow, but on the eight-year-old girl in the group, who's an experienced young rider out with her mother and aunt, the water comes up to her stirrups. I've crossed other rivers on horseback, but for BB Lookalike this is a first. He takes all of this in his stride.

As I'm busy exclaiming how wonderful it would be to ride out every day in unspoilt scenery with no cars, bikes or trucks to spook the horse, I hear a buzzing sound in the distance. The source of the disturbance appears to be coming from the river. The buzzing turns to a loud hum. Underneath me, my horse's body stiffens and he pulls his head up, ears pricked—the sign of an animal's flight instinct, which no amount of training, natural or otherwise, can subdue. A horse's ability to outrun a predator is crucial to its survival.

The noise turns into a dull roar, increasing in volume. I turn to see what the cause of the commotion can be. I've met mobility scooters, combine harvesters, giant tractors and noisy motorbikes when out riding a horse, but this is the first time I've encountered a jet boat.

The horse jogs on the spot, sensing danger. We are thirty metres away from the noisy boat. If he were to flee, I'd have very little control over him in a bitless bridle. I make a snap decision to turn him away from the noisy machine, by gently pulling him around, to face the other horses. Though he's still trembling, he drops his head as he turns towards the herd, who are far less agitated. He stops trotting on the spot and falls into an extended walk, reassured by their calming presence. As we head back to the yard, I feel him relax as he falls into line behind the others. I refuse to let the one hiccup spoil today's ride as I breathe in the mountain air for one last time.

But if I trek again, I'm going to lie about my experience and leave the horse with an overactive imagination to someone younger and fitter. Dope-on-a-rope all the way for me from now on.

11

The Accident-Prone
Accidental Plus One

It's five months before I get to ride another horse, back in England, at the riding school I've been going to since 2012. As I'm on an unfamiliar horse, I start in the dressage arena for a few sessions before I'm ready to hack out on Stockbridge Down. Owned by the National Trust, it's glorious riding country. I spot chalk hill blue butterflies and a pair of red kites. After ten weeks back in the saddle, I'm at the same level I was when we left in 2019.

Then life takes an unexpected turn.

It's Saturday 10 August 2024 and despite my eye mask, I'm awake at first light, which at this time of the year in the UK is around 5.30am. Three cups of tea and a shower later, I'm up and about. It seems daft to be thinking about such mundane things as checking my car tyres at this time of the morning, but in Australia, where people tend to get up earlier than in Britain, this wouldn't seem so strange.

The nearest supermarket, which opens at 7am, has a petrol station with an air compressor, and as there will be very few people around at this time on a Saturday, I won't have to queue. I can check the tyres and get the shopping done and be home by the time other people are just getting up. It's a gorgeous day and I can then take myself off for a walk, maybe across the fields to Hursley or further afield into the South Downs National Park.

I'm at the supermarket in five minutes as there's no school run to contend with nor cars waiting to get across the roundabout. I drive around the solitary car at the service station and pay for the air. And as I suspected, all the tyres needed inflating.

Once that chore is done, I jump back into the car and find a space in the supermarket carpark. I count no more than six cars. Feeling smug that I've beaten the rush, I grab my shopping bags and stride off, a spring in my step as I cross over towards the footpath.

When I put my right foot onto the path, it slides forward and sends me off balance. The momentum pushes my body forward and to the right. And now I'm falling. I put out my right hand on an angle, pinkie finger thumping the pavement in a failed effort to protect my right cheek as it smashes onto the ground. My hand takes the full impact of the fall, but the pain is coming from my face. It puffs up and I don't even need to look in a mirror to know I have a bruiser of a black eye.

An older couple come rushing to my aid and I'm escorted into the supermarket. They plonk me down on a bench seat, which, despite not being able to see properly, I can make out was donated in memory of a former employee. Angie, a member of staff who has pink hair and a raspy voice, spots me and runs for the First Aid box. The Duty Manager is called. A timid woman with an anxious expression, she stands awkwardly, encouraging her colleague, but doing nothing to assist.

Angie is more than capable of dealing with the situation on her own, wiping my face with an antiseptic cloth and putting a cold compress over my right eye, which is so swollen I can barely see out of it. My right hand is a mottled hue of reds and deep purples. A mother passing by holds her young daughter's hand tighter, the child pulling away from her, staring at me. I don't want to look in the mirror.

Even though I'm still in shock, I've worked out the reason for the Duty Manager's behaviour. She's terrified I'm going to take out a personal injury claim with one of those "no-win-no-fee" lawyers, or worse still, that I'll put a lousy rating about the supermarket on TripAdvisor. (My advice would be, wear different shoes and don't trip in the first place.) What she doesn't know is that in three weeks, I'll be back on a plane to Australia, and I have neither the time nor the energy to claim compensation.

I Fought the Pavement, and the Pavement Won

Angie calls a taxi company on my phone, handing it back to me when the despatcher asks where I'm going.

'A&E department at Winchester Hospital,' I tell him.

'When would you like that for?' he asks.

Seriously? Does he not know that A stands for accident and E for emergency?

'How about now?'

'It'll be 45 minutes,' the despatcher says.

'Okay,' I say. 'I'll have to wait then.' I turn to Angie. 'They can't get here for another 45 minutes.'

'Can I get you a coffee?' Angie asks. Not only does she go and fetch me a flat white, but she pays for it out of her own money. I offer to reimburse her, but she won't hear of it. Here she is, working the shop floor in a supermarket, probably being paid minimum wage, and she is buying me a coffee.

When all this is over, I'm going to get her a present.

A lady in her mid-seventies, who witnessed my fall, walks over and offers to take me to A&E. How kind. I gratefully accept, cancelling the cab as I walk out to the carpark with this compassionate stranger.

We're at the hospital in a little over five minutes. She drops me as close as she can, then walks in with me. Miracle upon miracles, I am the only patient in there. I give my personal details to the receptionist and take a seat in the empty waiting room.

The friendly young A&E doctor who comes to treat me takes one look at me and bursts out laughing.

'Sorry,' he says, 'but presenting with a black eye and a bruised right hook is a classic sign you've been in a fight.'

I play along. 'I did have a fight. With the pavement. I lost.'

I still can't believe that I'm the only patient, as this weekend the area is playing host to the Boomtown festival, Winchester's answer to Glastonbury. I expected to be crawling over comatose teenagers who'd popped one pill too many.

'It is Boomtown this weekend, right?' I ask the doctor.

'Yeah. But they've got a medical team on site. We had one or two in last night, along with everyone else. It was quite busy.'

'I'm lucky, then, aren't I?'

He examines my face. 'That depends on your definition of lucky. But yes, it looks a lot worse than it is. Nothing broken there. But I'm going to send you to X-ray for your wrist.'

'It feels okay,' I say. 'It was my face I was worried about.'

The doctor is insistent, so I do as I'm advised. At X-ray, I'm still the only patient and I'm soon finished there.

I head back to A&E. It doesn't take long for the result to come in.

'Not good news, I'm afraid,' the young doctor tells me. 'You've fractured your fifth metacarpal on your right hand.'

My medical knowledge is so limited, I process this news as, *it's only a fracture*, failing to understand that a fracture and a break are the same thing. Nonetheless, my face falls.

'It's your dominant hand, I take it?' he asks.

'Yes, the one I write with,' I say. All I can think about is that the book launch for *The Accidental Plus One* is exactly a month away.

He puts the injured hand in a brace and a sling, then refers me to the orthopaedic clinic. I get an appointment for Tuesday.

'Give it six weeks,' he says as I walk out the door in a daze.

'Thank you, that gives me hope,' I say, still in a state of shock.

Six weeks isn't so bad.

As I step out of A&E, I turn right, down Romsey Road towards Winchester, to catch a bus home. And then I remember that I was about to go shopping when disaster struck. I haven't had breakfast and there's no food in the house. Before I head home, I'm going to need to do a shop and buy enough food to last me until at least tomorrow.

As I walk down the hill, I phone a relative who's a former hand therapist.

'You won't manage at home on your own with one hand,' she tells me. I'm still in denial, as I don't yet know what I will and won't be able to do until I try. 'I'll come up tomorrow, and after you've had your hospital appointment on Tuesday, I'll drive you down here.'

'What would I do without you?'

We work out the logistics of the travel arrangements. She'll come by train and then drive me to Devon in my car. The same car that's stuck in the supermarket carpark. Angie promised she'd stick a note on it so that it doesn't get towed away, but I still need to get it home, even though I can't drive it. To complicate matters, it's electric, which is trickier to master compared with other cars. My relative is going to have her work cut out driving it from Hampshire to Devon.

But for now, I put that thought aside. My immediate needs are to grab some shopping and head home.

Living with One Hand

The nearest supermarket is a Co-op below the railway station, so I head down the hill in that direction. Unsurprisingly, what my relative told me turns out to be spot on. Shopping with one hand is awkward. I hold the basket in my left hand and my bag on the same shoulder.

I experiment by placing the basket in the crook of my right elbow joint so that I can grab the items I want with my good hand. I sling fresh filled pasta and pre-prepared vegetables into the basket, careful not to overfill it as my elbow joint isn't very strong and the two handles dig into my flesh. When I get to the counter and plonk the full basket down, I'm exhausted and it's only day one. Forty-one to go.

After spending ages packing the shopping so that I can carry it, I veto the bus. With only one functioning hand, getting on and off will be awkward. I walk up the hill to the railway station, where the waiting taxis are lined up. I'm home in less than 15 minutes.

I think about all the things I can do. I can still use my laptop and phone, even if I can only type with one hand, and there's always voice-activated software. It's only 10.15am. Three hours ago, I had all my limbs intact and was able to look after myself. And I hate asking for help. But my electric car isn't going to drive itself, so I post a picture of my hand in plaster to our local WhatsApp group, asking if one of my neighbours would be game enough to drive it back home. A former engineer volunteers. Another neighbour, who has a broken rib, offers to drive us up to the supermarket to fetch the car. It's an incredibly generous offer as he must be in a lot of pain.

When we get there, I do a quick explanation in the carpark, covering all the quirks of my car, and then we're off. I'm so lucky to have such wonderful neighbours. Once the car is parked outside the house, I relax.

I write my first text message with my left hand to let the riding club know what's happened. I'm paid up until the end of August, but won't be able to ride again now for at least a year. I'll miss it, but that's life.

I make myself a pot of tea in the afternoon, with my left hand doing all the heavy lifting. There's nothing else for it but to take it easy and read the newspapers for the rest of the day. At six o'clock, I pour myself a glass of wine. It's time to start making dinner.

I cook fresh meals, from scratch, nearly every night of the week. I have good knife skills, learnt the hard way by being shouted at in restaurant kitchens and told to start again when my mirepoix (diced vegetables) wasn't a uniform size. My right hand is, of course, my chopping hand. There's no way in the world I trust myself to chop an onion using my left hand. If I had to chop something, I concede I could just about manage a shallot, but anything bigger than that would guarantee me a return visit to A&E.

All I have to do is grate fresh parmesan and chop some parsley to go with the pre-cut broccoli, which I'm serving with the fresh pasta. I put a tea towel under the chopping board to keep it stable and try to use my left hand to do both jobs. Easier said than done. The "chopped" parsley is the size of the vegetables and my grating efforts are such a mess that I end up stabbing the parmesan into small pieces. The resulting mess would be an instant exit on *MasterChef*, but I'm the only one who sees it.

I manage to stay awake until 10.30pm, and then head upstairs where the fun bit starts, as I struggle to remove my clothing. I manage to get the shoulder straps off my bra and turn it around so that the clasp faces the front. After a couple of goes, I unhook it and collapse with exhaustion. I'm not looking forward to this ritual every night for the next six weeks. Maybe M&S will come up with a solution.

The next morning, I wake up early as usual and make my customary three cups of tea. As it's Sunday, I plan to walk across the water meadows to get the newspapers. But first, I find a couple of thick plastic bags and tie them around my strapped hand before cautiously getting into the shower. Luckily my hair doesn't need washing, so I don't have to try to do that with one hand yet.

In the middle of the afternoon, my rescuer arrives and we spend the rest of the day and all of Monday walking and packing, ready for our drive down to Devon on Wednesday. On Tuesday morning, I go to my appointment at the orthopaedic clinic. It's busy with young children who have fallen off scooters or out of trees. School holidays are the busiest times of year for the broken bones clinic, the consultant tells me. I come out of there with a shiny new white plaster and a further appointment in three weeks, just before my flight back to Australia.

International Terrorist?

If I'm stupid enough to fall over and break my dominant hand, summer is the best time of year to do it, as it forces me to have a holiday. I can't write, ride a horse or drive a car, so I make the most of all that seaside Devon has to offer from long walks, eating crab sandwiches on the quay at Salcombe and being driven to out-of-the-way pubs that only locals know about.

Before I fly back to Australia, I contact Singapore Airlines to tell them about my hand. The operator advises me that they can offer me wheelchair assistance, but as I am perfectly capable of walking, I decline. I merely take the precaution of changing my seat from a window on the left to one on the right-hand side of the plane, so that my broken wrist is protected from the other passengers in my row. Mindful about my one-night stop-over in Singapore, where I will need to lug my suitcase to and from a taxi and an airport shuttle bus, I'm strict about keeping the weight of my checked-in luggage well below my allowance, as 17kg is all I can comfortably carry in my left hand.

My flight is on Monday 2 September with a check-in at 6.35pm. At check-in, a kindly fellow passenger offers to lift my suitcase onto the scales. As I walk towards departure, a ground staff employee spots my hand in plaster and escorts me through passport control.

I could milk this one, if I wanted to. Let's see how far it gets me.

The answer is not very far.

At security, an officer regards my cast with suspicion.

'Can I cut off this cast, please? And look inside?'

What do you think I've got hidden in there? I wonder. *Drugs or diamonds, maybe?*

'No, you may not,' I say. 'I have a letter from my orthopaedic surgeon, explaining about the fracture and why my hand is in plaster. Do you want to see it?'

'No, no, it's alright, ma'am,' he says and ushers me through.

As I make my way to the gate, which is quite a hike, I notice the disabled seating area. Still in denial, I set off to sit down with the rest of the economy class passengers, but as it's standing room only, I turn around and head off back to the disabled seating.

I should qualify, I tell myself, even though the seats are reserved for priority boarding. But there's only one way to find out.

When the flight is called, the priority boarding queue is invited up first. I shuffle forward, and if I could cross my fingers, which are held rigid in my cast, I would. Sure enough, I'm ushered through before *any* of the privileged classes—first, business, platinum, or gold. Being first on board enables me to put my hand luggage up into the overhead bin, which I manage to do unassisted, then I squeeze over to my seat and snuggle up next to the window.

A Sikh gentleman in his mid-thirties, displaying a big yellow sticker on his tracksuit top, sits down at the end of my row. The sticker indicates his disability, but I can't read it from my seat. Surely, he can't be travelling on his own?

When a flight attendant comes over to check his ticket, I find out he doesn't speak any English. The flight attendant looks around for anyone who might be his carer. But nobody wants to claim him as their own. She asks in the surrounding rows, until an embarrassed family five rows back finally 'fesses up, saying that he belongs to them.

So, they just dumped him in my row, on his own, with no assistance, because they didn't want him next to them? Poor man, what mean relatives.

When a slight Singaporean girl, who can't be more than 19 or 20, turns up in my row, I'm relieved. And even more relieved when the exit row seat stays free for the entire 13-hour trip, now the unfortunate man has been reunited with his uncaring family. The girl is next to me in the middle seat. And the first thing she does is whip out her phone.

Probably looking at the latest video on TikTok.

But then she starts speaking, or is it chanting? I pretend to drop a tissue to see what she's really doing. It turns out she's reading Roman Catholic prayers on her phone, and from what I can see, they are all prayers to the Blessed Virgin.

She must be really scared of flying.

The only time she stops praying is during the meal service.

As it looks like it's going to be a long night if she carries on with the prayers, I break my self-imposed rule when flying long haul and order a glass of wine with dinner. But as soon as our trays are collected, my neighbour puts a blanket over her head, hiding her face, and snuggles down to sleep. I really want to ask her if she'd consider moving to the aisle seat so that we could both have more space, but before I have time, she's out cold. On my left shoulder.

I haven't the heart to tell her to move as she looks so young and vulnerable. But as our plane flies through the night, she snuggles up closer to me, like a large and affectionate dog, and wedges me into my seat. And as much as I try to push her away, I can't wake her. She just keeps creeping closer to me.

I give up on sleep and watch films back-to-back, then binge on box sets.

At Singapore, I manage the luggage to taxi transition with aplomb. I'm so tired after not sleeping on the plane that I am out like a light at 9pm. The room is quiet and dark, and as a result, I do what I never normally do and sleep in until 7.15am the next day. I am due downstairs with bags packed at 7.55am.

I grab the nearest plastic bag and tie up my right hand before jumping into the shower, then it's a mad scramble to get dressed one-handed, gather all my belongings and throw them into the suitcase, before sitting on the case to close it. On automatic pilot, I check the bathroom, safe and plug sockets for stray cables and chargers. Luckily my passports, wallet and phone are close to hand. By now it's 7.50am but I spend another 30 seconds doing another "idiot check," before grabbing my bag, closing the door and racing for the lift and down to get to reception to give my key back. The airport shuttle is waiting outside with its engine running.

Once on the shuttle, I relax. At least the Security Officer in Singapore is more on the ball than the one at Heathrow and asks if he can test my cast for explosives.

'Sure,' I say, 'as long as it's okay that my hand stays inside.' He gets his magic wand out and doesn't find anything on my person likely to blow up a plane.

At Melbourne, the pre-ordered taxi is there to meet me. When I arrive at Faulty Towers—a play on the classic British comedy *Fawlty Towers* and the name we have given our apartment block—BB Lookalike is waiting for me, ready to carry my big suitcase up nine flights of stairs. The lift has been out of action for the past three months, with two more months to go until it's fixed.

Faulty Towers indeed.

12

Faulty Towers

When we moved into our apartment, there were rumours that the single lift's days were numbered. It wasn't calibrated to be level on the upper floors and one elderly tenant in a wheelchair had great difficulty getting in and out of it. However, many of the owners were retirees on fixed incomes who refused to cough up for anything beyond basic maintenance.

The state of the lift soon took a backseat as more immediate issues began to affect us. We'd been here barely three weeks when the weather took a dramatic turn and dropped from a steamy 30C down to 12C in less than half an hour. The wind direction changed from north to south as angry-looking white-capped waves hurtled towards the beach, the sky darkened, thunder rumbled and the Eureka tower was illuminated in flashes of forked lightning.

We had front row seats to this sound and light spectacle. And then the rain started. A few drops built to a crescendo, like a tropical downpour in Singapore's wet season. From the coast, this rain came at us horizontally, forcing its way through the west-facing windows in the open-plan dining and sitting rooms. It pushed under the frames and saturated the sills and the wall directly below the windows.

We rushed to stem the flow, mopping up the deluge with towels, but couldn't keep up. We did what we could to protect the Landlord's floor and her shiny beige curtains, which were thirty years old at least, struggling to prop them up on our chairs to dry off as they weighed a ton.

When the rain was over, I examined the curtains. They were heavily lined, but smelled musty and were speckled with spots of mildew and mould. I let the Agent know about the leaks. She sent a handyman around and he put a sticking plaster on the problem by sealing up one of the windows so that it could no longer be opened from the inside. All this did was ensure that we couldn't ventilate the sitting room, unless we had the balcony door open.

And every time there was another leak, the Real Estate Agent sent around the same handyman. In March 2020, during the first Covid lockdown, the problem was considered a necessary repair and the handyman was granted permission to enter our property, provided all three of us were masked up.

The sticking plaster solution lasted for a few weeks until the next storm and once again the handyman came, spraying silicone around the window frames. But no matter how many times we reported the problem, the building's Managing Agent deflected all our enquiries and refused to take responsibility.

Our Real Estate Agent moved on, and when her replacement took over, she put pressure on the Managing Agent until they sent a plumber who inspected the problem. Then there was radio silence for another two years, until in 2023, the Owners' Corporation finally appointed an outside consultant to investigate the leaks as we weren't the only complainants. The Consultant suggested a more expensive sticking plaster approach, involving blokes armed with silicon glue guns hanging off the side of our roof on ropes, injecting the outside walls with sealant.

This second sticking plaster worked for 18 months, until January 2025 when a storm identical to the one five years before created another waterfall inside the apartment. Just like last time, we mopped up the leaks and propped up the replacement curtains on chairs. But, after five years, we'd got problem-reporting fatigue. Soon it would no longer be our problem and we decided to keep quiet.

If our previous complaints about the leaks had led to a solution that worked, we—and our neighbours—would have had no need to report anything anyway.

———

Lift Repair

In May 2024, because of an upcoming safety inspection, the Management Committee was forced to replace the original 1960s lift. When the place was built, the tight-fisted owners, who were young and sprightly back then, were too mean to pay for a second lift and we got two sets of stairs instead.

The lift replacement was scheduled to take four months, but in protest at the length of time it was going to take, a tenant on our floor gave her notice.

'No way am I walking up nine flights of stairs for four months,' she said. A couple, also on our floor, who were at least ten years younger than us, subsequently moved to the second floor as they couldn't cope with the climb.

'It's alright for you and BB Lookalike,' the woman told me. 'You're both young and fit.' I saved her blushes by not telling her how old we were, but BB Lookalike and I dined out on this story for weeks.

The cynic in me assumed that the Owners' Corporation chose the cheapest (and slowest) quote. I was away for part of the repair works so only had to endure two-and-a-half months without the lift as it took them longer than they promised. Unfortunately, this meant dragging a big suitcase down the stairs when I travelled to the UK in late May. We did this on the night of our wedding anniversary on our way out to dinner to celebrate. I padlocked my case to a railing at the back of the building as I had an early start the next day.

This was nothing compared with what BB Lookalike had to endure when he returned from his three-week holiday in the UK in June. After a 24-hour long-haul flight, he dragged his suitcase up to the ninth floor, where he was confronted by all our storage boxes, which had lived undisturbed in our storeroom next to the lift since January 2020, now piled up on the stairwell. It was after hours and everyone at the Management Company had gone home.

The next morning, as it was a working day, he went to the storeroom to get his bicycle. But his key wouldn't fit the lock. Puzzled, he asked the guys working on the lift what was going on.

'That room's ours now. We're working in there. You can't go in, mate,' one of the tradies said defensively.

'I'm looking for my bicycle,' BB Lookalike said. 'It was locked in this room.' The tradies glanced at each other.

'There were two bikes, right? We've put them on the roof for you,' one of them said.

'You've put two bicycles on the roof? It's winter. They'll rust up there.'

'It's alright, mate, I've put a tarp over them,' the tradie said, shrugging.

'I'm going to go up there and get them,' BB Lookalike said.

'No, mate, you're not allowed up there. Because of the asbestos. I'll get them down for you.'

After this bizarre conversation, BB Lookalike wasted half the morning when he should have been on campus, chasing up the Management Company. When he phoned me in the UK and told me this tale, I reminded him about the weird email we'd got from the company a few weeks back, asking us if we used our storeroom. We replied, telling them yes, it was full of our belongings, and that we had exclusive use of it as it was owned by our Landlord. Why, we wanted to know, were they asking?

In response, they ghosted us.

When BB Lookalike finally did get through, the Management Company told him the tradies had broken into the storeroom and changed the lock as it was "common property" and they needed to put all the electrical cabling in that room. BB Lookalike sent an email in response and copied in our Real Estate Agent, who hadn't been notified either, so that she could forward this interesting "fact" to the Landlord.

Subsequently, emails flew backwards and forwards between the Management Company, the Landlord and the Real Estate Agent. We stayed out of it, cheered up by the fact that the Landlord and Real Estate Agent were fighting our corner. The Landlord had the most to lose, as she had owned the property for over 30 years, at least 20 years longer than the current agents had been "managing" the building. According to the title deeds, it looked very much like she was in the right and the Managing Agent was wrong. And her daughter, who had power of attorney, was a lawyer.

Whatever the outcome, we were unlikely to have a

storeroom any time soon. Our boxes stayed firmly put in the stairwell, as we had nowhere else to store them, and they remained there until the week before our tenancy came to an end.

I found out later that the lift repairs went to a company that took the job on the understanding the tradies would work in "downtime", which was evenings, weekends and public holidays. No wonder it took them five months to complete it.

Rising Damp

When we first moved in, we never gave a moment's thought to where our hot water came from, other than out of the tap. We last rented an apartment in 2017 in Boston during the fall semester (autumn term), where all the heating and hot water was communal. When we signed up for this latest tenancy, we were pleased there was a heating and cooling system, but there was no mention of hot water.

At the start of 2022, we notice a musty smell of mould coming from our kitchen, specifically on the side wall in the pantry, and in the hallway. However, it isn't until the downstairs neighbours complain of leaks seeping through their ceiling that we are contacted by our Real Estate Agent. She sends a plumber who worked on the apartment when our elderly Landlord lived here. When he arrives, he takes one look at the lino in the kitchen, which is lifting because of the damp, then inspects the pantry wall.

'It's the hot water tank,' he announces.

'What hot water tank?'

'The one in the hot water cupboard, next to the pantry.'

'There's a hot water cupboard?' *You'd have to be Miss Marple to find it*, I think.

I open the pantry door. Sure enough, the white chip-board floor-to-ceiling panel on the left-hand side has a series of screws in it. Removable ones.

'Behind that wall,' the plumber says.

'Seriously? So, every time something goes wrong with the boiler, we have to move all of this,' I say, pointing to the five shelves, laden with enough essential (and non-essential) ingredients for the next six months. 'Is this the only way?'

'Afraid so. I installed that hot water tank 20 years ago and it's likely it's got to the end of its life.'

BB Lookalike helps me move all the contents of the pantry, which we line up on the dining room table in rows so that we can put the things back in the same order, while the plumber removes all the screws and places the panel onto the kitchen floor. If this was a movie, an apartment with hidden panels would reveal a safe containing used bank notes, a key to a secret vault or priceless jewels. In real life, there is a grubby old appliance and a dirty wet floor to mop.

'As I thought. The old Rheem hot water tank has burst,' he says. 'It'll need replacing. I'll call the Agent now to tell her as you'll need a new one.'

Fortunately, our Real Estate Agent contacts the owner straight away to get the go ahead to buy the new tank. The plumber secures a replacement that day and installs it later on in the afternoon.

But the fun doesn't stop there. Even though the hot water tank is new, it is temperamental as a year later, we hear beeping coming from the cupboard. You know the drill: call the Agent, explain the problem, and out comes the same plumber who installed it.

'That's the battery on the boiler, it needs replacing every year,' he tells us. Funny he failed to mention that last year when he installed the new boiler.

'So, we've got to take out all the shelves every year just to replace the battery?' I ask, hoping I've misunderstood. 'And we can't do this ourselves?'

'No, I'll have to do it,' the plumber says. I set the stopwatch on my phone and time how long it takes him to do the job. He is in and out in nine minutes.

Nice work if you can get it, I think, curious as to how much he'll be charging for a call-out and nine minutes' work. But as the Landlord will be paying this bill, I won't ever get to find out.

Near Misses

Every week, or so it seems, the fire brigade is called out to investigate alarms in two buildings lining the beach, which we can see from our front windows. One is a restaurant, the Stokehouse, which burned down ten years ago and had to be completely rebuilt. Because the fire alarm in that building is so sensitive, we've nicknamed it the Smokehouse. And the other building where the smoke alarm regularly goes off is another restaurant, right next to my gym.

I'm in my early morning Pilates class, feeling smug for getting to the gym so early, when the fire alarm goes off in the building next door. We evacuate, but I make sure I have my phone, my bag and my shoes. As we wait around outside for the fire brigade to turn up, I'm thankful that it's summer, and that I wasn't in the swimming pool. There are folks here in their bathers, a towel wrapped around their waist.

We're allowed back into the class ten minutes later and the teacher kindly makes up the time so that we won't miss out. As the fire alarms going off in one or other of the two restaurants is such a common occurrence, I think nothing more of this, until one Saturday afternoon when we are at home. A fire alarm shrieks, and this time, it's much closer than either of the usual suspects.

'It's in this building,' BB Lookalike says as the siren gets louder and louder. I run down the hallway and grab our passports, sling my laptop into my bag, snatch up my phone, and we head out the door.

'Let's take the back staircase as it's the official fire exit,' I say. We make our way down the nine flights as quickly as we can with me holding the handrail. It's five months since I fractured my wrist and I'm still having hand therapy to improve my grip strength.

The last thing I need is another fall.

As we reach floor 3, a guy yells, 'Evacuate the building, now. Everyone out.' When we get to the ground floor, Action Man is there already, directing us out the back of the building to the carpark, where a woman I recognise as someone who recently moved in is holding a cat carrier containing a blue-eyed Burmilla cat with silver fur. The cat looks remarkably calm and not even the least bit bothered, even though it's 38C and the sun is blazing.

Action Man turns out to be her partner.

'He's ex-Special Forces,' she says. As we are talking, Action Man runs back into the building. And in a blink, there he is on the third-floor balcony, fire extinguisher in hand, spraying the fire, which is coming from a faulty air-conditioner that has blown up. He appears robot-like, on automatic pilot with no thought for his own safety. As he tackles the fire, he's enveloped by a cloud of grey smoke and starts to cough. He wraps a scarf around his mouth, but this is no match for the toxic fumes pouring out of the appliance.

Then, fire engines arrive. A lot of fire engines.

Four? I think. And all the firies are wearing breathing apparatus, while Action Man has tackled the blaze in a pair of shorts, a t-shirt and flip-flops. He comes out of the building and walks past the gates, holding his hand to his mouth and coughing. He doesn't look well, so he should really have waited for the firies with all the right equipment to arrive.

The fire on the third floor is not the only potential disaster that has to be averted during our time in St Kilda. One Sunday, as we are stepping out of the building, we hear something crashing to the ground behind us. We jump out the way, narrowly escaping being hit by what appears to be lumps of masonry. I look up to see which floor they came from. The second-floor balcony, by the looks of it. I text the couple who own the apartment, who are currently away. The woman replies, saying she's reported the loose masonry and they won't let their dog onto the balcony until it's fixed. She warns us that there are similar defects on all the other floors and advises us to check our apartment.

When we get home, I inspect our balconies, thanking my lucky stars we never bought here.

Repairs

A month before we move out, the Real Estate Agent asks if there's any work that needs doing before she advertises the property to new tenants. This is a canny move, as it saves her the bother of coming around to see for herself.

I remind her about a cracked window next to the

dining area. From the day we moved in, we've been stressing that it needs fixing. By the first six-monthly inspection, it was mid-winter and as the southerly storms blew in, we were scared that the window would do the same. But by then, it was the middle of the Covid lock-downs, so our Real Estate Agent was working from home and only emergency repairs were being authorised.

At the second and subsequent sixth-monthly property inspections, we mentioned the cracked window, until here we are, five-and-a-half-years later, with it still not fixed. It may be that the Agent tried to get the Landlord to repair it but was turned down. But a friend was so frightened the window was going to fall out that she sealed it with duct tape. And that tape stays put until it is time for us to give our notice.

And then, like magic, a glazier appears. Along with a blinds and curtains specialist to measure up for blinds in our bedroom to replace the venerable, flowery master-bedroom curtains. We've tolerated them for five years as, although they're daggy, they're lined and keep out the worst of the howling gales.

The simplest and cheapest renovation I suggest—redecorating the main bathroom ceiling—appears to have been ignored. As we want all of the nearly $5,000 deposit back, we touch up the ceiling ourselves.

In 2024, the rent went up by $100 a week, but we negotiated a 50% discount for the five months the lift was out of action. By the time we left in 2025, we were paying $850 a week and there was no storage room.

Despite its quirks, the eccentric building we live in has a real sense of community with a diverse range of tenants. There are renters who come and go living side by side with the owner-occupiers. Our neighbours across the hall are a delightful young couple from Dublin who have come to

Australia on the Working Holiday Visa. As the apartment has been let with no furniture, I give them as much crockery as I can spare. In return, they give us a leg of lamb from the farm where the man works.

Who gets the better deal? I'll let you decide. But the lamb was delicious.

13

In My 'Hood

The official start of summer in St Kilda is as soon as it is warm enough outside at night for the various tribes that invade our neighbourhood to venture onto the street and make some noise. It could be as early as November and run until the middle of March, coinciding with two major events: the Melbourne Grand Prix and the St Kilda Festival.

Each year, Albert Park, less than a mile from where we live, is leased out to Liberty Media, a publicly traded entertainment company, to run a Formula 1 race. The terms of the lease allow the company to close off the park to the public for ten days before and after the race. Not having any interest in motor sport, I watch the event on television for the first time in 2025. Even I can see that there must be an element of schadenfreude among the spectators, many of whom I suspect are waiting for a professional driver to slip up.

In the days leading up to the final race before we leave St Kilda in 2025, we are treated to an impromptu aerobatics display as a stunt pilot practises his moves over the waters of Port Phillip Bay, right in front of our apartment. The weather conditions are perfect—bright, sunny and still, with visibility as far as the You Yangs and Macedon mountain ranges, Geelong, and the Mornington Peninsula. I will the flyer to execute his precision moves safely and am enthralled when he loops the loop, flies upside down, dives from a great height, and then recovers his aircraft in a straight line before climbing again and repeating the same manoeuvre.

In 2020 and 2021, thanks to Covid 19, there was no Grand Prix, so when it returned in 2022, we stayed put instead of getting out of town, like many locals do. The disruption started on Thursday with the 96 tram cancelled and replaced by a bus, which took nearly an hour to get into the city as it went on a magical mystery tour, past the Grand Prix track and various places in South Melbourne I never knew existed. Our weekly circular walk to Prahran Market, which usually took us past Albert Park Lake, was blocked off so we had to return the way we'd just come.

On Friday, the buzz of helicopters flying directly over-head built to a crescendo, and by Sunday, the day of the race, I'd timed the take-offs and landings to be every 30 seconds. From our kitchen window, we could see one of the helipads, which its operator boasted "is right next to the racetrack at Gate 10". Its website suggested that, to avoid all the traffic, "why not fly to the Grand Prix?" From our apartment, it sounded like everybody had done exactly that.

As well as spectators, the helicopters ferried drivers, along with their entourages and lightweight equipment, to and from the race venue. Is there a clause in the drivers' contracts that no one else is allowed to drive them in a car and only a helicopter will do? This didn't go down well with the locals who had zero interest in motor racing and were concerned about the environmental impact of the sport.

Formula 1 sends all its cars, fuel, personnel and fans by plane to 21 countries across four continents: Asia, Europe, North America and Oceania. The CO2 generated by F1 is equivalent to the amount generated on the island of Tonga (population 104,600) in the whole of 2023. For the next three years of our time in St Kilda, we leave town on Grand Prix weekend, swapping the noise and traffic for rural Victoria.

___

Festivals

Out of the three big music festivals that directly impact us, the St Kilda Festival, held over a weekend in the middle of February, is the most disruptive. It's not because we don't like the music—the first year it was back after Covid, we hosted a party so that friends could see the Hoodoo Gurus, an iconic Australian band formed in the 80s, as the stage was directly opposite our building, across the road on the grassed area in front of the beach.

But there's a downside of our free musical treat. The clean-up after the event goes on all night long on the Sunday, the council employing what we call "the sadistic street cleaners" and arming them with rubbish trucks equipped with loud beeps and a big booming robot voice that announces the vehicle is reversing, which no amount of noise-cancelling earplugs can mute. They may as well broadcast it through a loud hailer, so that anyone who was asleep will be guaranteed to be awoken and stay that way until 5am.

After one experience of this, we decide to go away for the weekend of the St Kilda Festival in future.

The Foreshore Festival, held in the carpark next to the Palais Theatre, takes place from the end of February to mid-March. Live bands play on a specially constructed stage over seven nights across three weekends. We don't tend to go away for this one as we enjoy free gigs from some high-quality acts, including British band The Kooks and Ireland's Fontaines DC. If a band we like is performing, we get value out of our $850 a week rent as tickets to these gigs sell for $115 each. And just like the St Kilda Festival, the festival-goers have to stand, use Portaloos and pay to buy expensive food and drink, while we lounge about on comfortable sofas, raiding the fridge whenever we want to replenish our drinks and eating proper food, as well as having exclusive access to clean bathrooms we don't have to queue for.

I know which one I prefer.

Motorbike Tuesdays, Bongo Night Thursdays and Wailing Sundays

Every Tuesday, without fail, at around 7pm, there's a steady stream of motorbike riders driving along the Esplanade, like noisy hornets. They are the Melbourne Street Riders and their Facebook group has over 16,000 members. Obviously, they don't all descend on the Palais carpark opposite us. But those who do, hang about for half an hour, showing off their bikes to the easily impressed, before moving off in a convoy.

In the first week of February 2025, Victorian Opera stages Stephen Sondheim's *Follies* at the Palais Theatre and we have tickets for the Tuesday 4 February performance. As the show doesn't start until 7.30pm, we gather outside the Palais at 7.15, ready to take our seats. But the traffic division of Victoria Police is there before us, waiting for the Melbourne Street Riders.

When they arrive for their weekly gathering, they seem nonplussed that the Palais is a working theatre and not just a meeting place for entitled bikers. The police move them on just in time for curtain up, to our relief. The last thing that we ticket holders want to hear when we're about to enjoy a show we've paid good money for is backfiring motorbikes.

Once we've got Motorbike Tuesdays out the way, we get one night off from street noise. But on Thursdays, starting at sundown, St Kilda Drumming and its merry band of bongo players give us an informal, and not exactly welcome, performance. In a trance-like state, they drum away the evening, sometimes going on until 11pm. Bongo Thursdays are meant to be held at Catani Gardens, a kilometre west of us, but a group of drummers prefers to bang away right opposite our building. We drown out the monotonous thumping with our own playlists or turn the TV up to mask the noise.

For the organisers and participants of these two noise-making activities, St Kilda is a great place to go for a night out. But those of us that live in the community—kids, shift workers and the 9-to-5 crowd—are entitled to a decent night's sleep, especially on a school night.

Weekends, though, the gloves are off. On Friday and Saturday nights, we do hear the commotion of large groups of people seemingly on a mission to get as drunk as humanly possible, plus an occasional Air Ambulance helicopter flying over our building in the middle of the night, but we usually manage to go back to sleep. Not so on Sunday when the street cleaners start at 5.30am. They must either be deaf and not realise how much noise they are making or enjoy waking as many people as possible at the crack of dawn.

The Sunday clean-up is a little different from the St Kilda Festival one as the cleaners start by doing wheelies around the Palais Theatre carpark. Then it's the turn of the Esplanade itself, where they operate an especially loud machine that cleans the tram tracks until they're so shiny, you could see your reflection in them.

Once the street cleaners have been and gone, the stall-holders for the regular St Kilda Esplanade Sunday Market set up. Known as a Makers' Market, it sells a range of arts, crafts and, more recently, street foods, which include a coffee concession, Dutch pancakes, Mexican tacos and Vietnamese takeaways.

Buskers make a beeline for the market and set up their guitars and portable amps right in front of our building. We nicknamed one notably bad busker that plagued us for a few months over summer Wail-on Jennings, not to be confused with the American singer-songwriter Waylon Jennings. Unlike the real artist, fake Wail-on's repertoire is limited to the most mournful tunes he can find on the internet. After listening to themes of drug overdoses, divorce, betrayal and going to prison, all sung off key and accompanied by a string of bum notes and shrieking feed-back from Wail-on's guitar, we decide our best option, before we lose the will to live, is to leave the apartment and go somewhere—anywhere—else.

All That Glitters

The contrasts between the different tribes of St Kilda are more apparent to me on Sundays than any other day of the week. Perhaps it's because I have more time to study them on a weekend.

Old St Kilda is represented by the immigrant communities who moved to Melbourne post-war. For the past 45 years, the same Greek family has run the newsagent on the corner of Acland and Fitzroy Street. And for five-and-a-half years, I've been one of their customers. I buy newspapers in their shop a couple of times a week. I could get these from either of the two supermarkets in St Kilda, but I prefer the human interaction in this little corner store.

At first, I was served by the patriarch who emigrated to Australia from Greece. He was a gentle, kind man, who I once witnessed calling an ambulance for one of the local drug addicts who was sparked out, comatose right outside his shop. Sadly, the patriarch died during Covid and his elderly widow took over the shop. I only knew he'd died because the shop was closed while the family attended his funeral. I expressed my condolences and his wife thanked me by giving me a couple of Lindt chocolates.

Although I have never seen the elderly lady dressed in anything but mourning black, she greets every single customer cheerfully. She now runs the shop with her son, who is a second-generation Greek-Australian. I admire her for coming to work, instead of being on her own at home.

When I go into the shop today, a glazier is busy replacing the glass door, which has been smashed by an intruder. The son tells me that it is only the fourth time in 45 years that this has happened, two of the break-ins occurring in the past two years

What's wrong with people?

I don't know many businesses that have had a connection with the area for as long as this family-run shop. Contrast this with the corporate property developers of St Kilda, who are only interested in making money. Hardly surprising they flock here as it's a place where a high-end apartment can sell for $30+ million. In the building three doors down from us, the penthouse apartment was bought for $33 million, and in May 2025 was put up for sale for $36 million. The Real Estate Agent listed it on Facebook and made the mistake of allowing comments. This is a selection of the best:

'Gold Coast naff. Interior needs gutting and rebuilding.'

'Six bedrooms! Geeze, some people must do a lot of breeding.'

'The only people who live in that building have fake tits and trout pouts!'

The over-the-top Saint Moritz complex, designed for bling-enthusiasts, has a bar, cinema, gym, library, 24-hour concierge, 25-metre indoor pool, yoga room, valet parking and private working spaces known as chairman's lounges. The in-house Samsara Anti-aging & Wellness Retreat offers a range of luxurious treatments, including salt rooms, plunge pools, saunas and a spa with a floatation pod. And—wait for it—a cryogenic chamber, according to the Real Estate Agent's advertising material.

Travel show presenter Anthony Bourdain tried out cryotherapy in his documentary series *Parts Unknown* when he visited Nashville. He didn't last long in the tank. If residents of the building want full immersion in extremely low temperatures, all they need do is walk across the road from their apartment to Port Phillip Bay. Also known as the sea.

The building has had a chequered history in the three years since it was completed. The many high-profile owners, including a billionaire, have been loud in voicing their concerns, especially about defects. The private dispute spilled out into the press, when one investor accused the property developer of trying to hide the poor quality construction. Other owners who have reported problems, according to one insider, had to sign non-disclosure agreements to get them rectified.

In January 2025, the *Financial Review* included a piece stating that an apartment for sale with alleged construction defects in the rich-listers' Saint Moritz development had dropped in price by $1.3 million compared to what the owners bought it for in 2022. In an attempt at damage control, the developers tried to pass off the problems with the construction as mere snagging items, common to every new build. Then they boasted at how many problems they'd resolved, throwing in some dubious statistics. But no amount of talking-up their successes mitigated the fact that there were still ongoing problems, even after the 12-month post-settlement defect period. Rich owners, it would seem, have deep pockets and are not afraid of taking legal action to put things right.

The restaurant space on the ground floor has had its own unique set of problems too. The first restaurant to lease the space was Loti. I never understood the name, as I kept misreading it as Loki, the shapeshifter from Nordic mythology. After the restaurant closed, I discovered that the name is actually an acronym for Lady of the Ice.

It turns out that everyone else was confused about the restaurant's concept too, which is probably why it closed. In one article, it was described as a "high-end seafood restaurant" (complete with a high-end ex-Noma chef, Elijah Holland). I read elsewhere it was both a fine diner and an all-day cafe with a kitchen featuring curing, fermentation, flame and smoke. The chef claimed he liked to forage for local and wild ingredients.

Where does he intend to go foraging around here? I wondered. If he tried the beach before the cleaners got there, all he'd find were used condoms and syringes. The closest I've got to foraging locally is pinching some rosemary off the bushes outside Luna Park, but I make sure I give it a good wash first. The trams, peeing dogs, peeing humans and goodness knows how many diesel and petrol cars going past probably coat it in something unmentionable.

In the same article, the chef expressed the desire for customers to come in any day of the week and find something new. I did try, but every time I walked past the restaurant, it never appeared to be open.

In March 2024, a Carlton institution, D.O.C., took on the lease and brought its popular brand to St Kilda. A high-end Italian pizzeria and pasta restaurant that offers takeaways, this has become our go-to as it's only 200 steps from our block. As of May 2025, the restaurant is still going strong. But we don't take its longevity for granted as since we've lived here, St Kilda always seems to be on the cusp of a great culinary revival, but so many restaurants have come and gone.

Even casual eateries struggle around here. Takeaway Claw & Tail opened in what was previously an ice-cream kiosk near the beach. An arm of the seafood catering outfit Oystertainers, Claw & Tail offered items like fish and chips as well as lobster rolls. It closed in March 2025, with the owners citing family commitments, but in all honesty, a venue like this is seasonal. There can't be much call for a pricy lobster roll in June, July and August. Maybe the increase in the cost of living means that more people are staying home and spending what money they have on their pets.

Post Pandemic Pets

On a train journey over Easter 2025, a couple sits near to us with the sweetest baby who doesn't cry once for the entire hour-and-a-half they are with us. Their dog, on the other hand, is a whining nightmare. Small dogs are permitted on long-distance trains in Victoria, provided they are kept in a pet carrier. This one isn't. It is a nervous wreck, shaking and yapping at its owner, demanding attention.

As passengers walk by, frowning at the whining dog, the man comes out with a string of excuses.

'She hates the vibration of the train, that's why she barks,' he says, by way of an apology.

I diagnose the problem as jealousy. They must have got the dog first, and when the baby was born, its nose was put well and truly out of joint as it was no longer the centre of their world. Except the dad hasn't got the memo. While the mother is cradling the baby, the dog gives a masterclass in attention-seeking behaviour, until the father picks it up and cuddles it.

According to research by Animal Medicines Australia, a fifth of all pet dogs in the country were obtained during the pandemic by both new and experienced owners. It's easy to understand why people would crave hanging out with a companion animal during lockdown. But post-pandemic, when employees were asked to return to the office, there was an immediate problem of what to do with Fido during the working day.

The problem was compounded for city dogs, especially those whose owners lived in apartments. Not only might the dog suffer from separation anxiety, but there was an immediate practical problem about where it was meant to relieve itself. This is where professional dog walkers spotted a gap in the market, charging \$25–\$35 for a group walk, or \$50 per hour for a dedicated solo dog walk. And I reckon most of them are in Melbourne, with over seven profes-sional dog walking companies in my area alone.

As I walk past the carpark at my local park, a van packed with barking dogs pulls up. The driver gets out of the van and opens up the back door. Dogs of every size, colour and age run out into the park. They charge around, some playing chase with each other, others happy to sniff their way past every tree. I don't see much evidence of any dog walking, as the person with them stays in the middle of the grassed area, chatting to all the other professional dog walkers. The dogs look happy, though, no doubt thrilled to have a distraction from being stuck at home while their owners are at work.

Occasionally, I'll encounter a walker from one of these companies on the bike path in the park with up to nine dogs. From there, they make their way over to the grassed area, and the first thing they do is let all the dogs off their leads. On the one hand, I don't blame them. One person can't be expected to control nine dogs, especially when the RSPCA recommends a maximum of four dogs per person. However, I do wonder how happy the owners would be if there was any footage of their dogs being walked in such large groups. Perhaps they aren't expecting their dogs to get one-on-one attention, and I suppose at least their dog has a social life.

14

Escapes to the Country

There are only so many parks and gardens I can walk around, even in Melbourne, which has some lovely ones, before I yearn for wide open spaces. Only 40km but a world away are chalets within the grounds of the Eastern Golf Club at Yering in the Yarra Valley, featuring abundant wildlife quite literally hopping past your living room window. There are beautiful forested areas where even on weekends, you might meet five people at most. Bliss compared with the city, where food delivery drivers ride their bikes on the pavement and entitled joggers overtake on the inside lane.

The chalets are well designed and spaced 50 metres apart for maximum privacy. Their decks are equipped with a table, chairs and a Weber barbecue. And on the inside, you'll find a king-sized bed, a spa bath, white waffle dressing gowns and slippers. The people who run the place even provide a continental breakfast hamper as the nearest shop is a ten-minute drive away.

The first time we came was Grand Prix weekend in 2023. As we don't have a car, we planned to do the trip on public transport, but we did have to go and pick the year of a major construction project to improve safety at level crossings. The tram and train journey took two-and-a-half hours.

The Uber pick up from Lilydale train station was smooth, but the return journey on the Sunday was anything but. Finding a taxi in the Yarra Valley at any time is hard enough. Finding one on Grand Prix weekend is impossible. In the end we had to call a friend who lives about 20km away to come to our rescue.

Roos in the Rain

On our second visit, we'd wised up that a car is essential when visiting the Yarra Valley. We again took the train to Lilydale, where the hire car was waiting, or rather the SUV, as we'd been upgraded. It was a VW Tiguan, a vehicle I'd never driven before, so I took it 200 metres from the rental car office and pulled in next to a coffee shop. Fortified by a skinny flat white, I set off with BB Lookalike for Healesville, the nearest market town, to stock up on provisions for our self-catering chalet.

The weather was misbehaving, so instead of taking the back road to Healeseville, I chanced it on the two-lane Maroondah Highway. So there I was, driving the automatic Tiguan, knowing where Drive and Reverse were; how to operate the windscreen wipers, the indicators and the lights. But no amount of random button pressing as I was driving along solved the mystery of the retractable side mirrors.

We made it to Healesville in one piece. Failing to find a parking space on the street, I located the nearest supermarket, guaranteed to have a carpark. We dumped the car, meandered up the street and discovered a gourmet food store, where we grabbed some fresh food for the barbecue. We then wandered down to the vegetable shop, where the produce was all locally sourced and much fresher than we'd find on any supermarket shelf.

Realising we hadn't had any lunch, we made our way to a branch of Beechworth Bakery and spotted a Kiwi classic—a steak and cheese pie. The weather forecast was predicting a drop in temperature from 30 degrees Celsius to anything between 11 and 17, with heavy showers alternating with sunshine, so I didn't need any more excuse for ordering a hearty pie. I got so carried away, I even asked for tomato sauce.

As we sat on a park bench eating our lunch, it started to rain. Neither spots nor drops, this was a steady downpour. We reluctantly moved from our seats and huddled in a doorway to finish off the last remaining morsels of crispy pastry and chunky fillings.

As the weather remained iffy on the Saturday, we stayed local and hiked along the river near the golf course. We spotted mobs of kangaroos at every turn, some grazing, others lolling under trees, all staring at us interlopers in their territory. Although the local golfers would be accustomed to having their swing criticised by random marsupials, it must be a novelty for international visitors.

Water, Water Everywhere

On Sunday, we opted to drive to the Christmas Hills for a walk at the Sugarloaf Reservoir.

'Let's do a circuit,' I said. 'It can't take more than a couple of hours.' By the time we saw the sign that said five hours and 18km, we were 3.5km in. Normal people who were ill-provisioned for a five-hour hike would have turned around. Not us numpties.

Before we left home the previous day, I'd mentioned we should take a water bottle with us, but in our eagerness to get going, we left it behind. The golf club charged $6 for a bottle of still water and I was too mean to pay it. So stupid us, we had no water and we were intent on completing another 15.5km to finish our walk.

A couple coming in the opposite direction said that there was only one significant hill ahead, and that made our minds up. We set off. The weather was 15C and there were frequent showers. As I walked along, I touched the damp leaves of plants I knew weren't poisonous and licked the moisture from those, but 9km in I became dry-mouthed and was wondering if we'd make it. The irony, of course, was that we were at a reservoir, where all of Melbourne's drinking water comes from.

And there are two carparks and a toilet block. Surely, they'll have drinking water?

But no such luck, as the water has to be treated before it can be drunk.

Just as I was thinking that if we got desperate, we could try our luck with untreated reservoir water, bushland suddenly gave way to heathland, covered in clumps of wild blackberries. Even though there had been very little rain, apart from the past two days, February is peak blackberry season. The berries were tiny, but amazingly sweet. We ate maybe a dozen each, which was enough to quench our thirst and give us energy for the last 9km.

Despite the blackberries' sustenance, at 14km, I hit a wall. My feet were aching and every uphill step was an effort. I wanted to stop for a rest, but if I did, I'd never get up again.

As I trudged up the hill, willing myself on, I spotted

parked cars. We must have taken a different track as we'd managed to slice 2km off our walk and were back where we'd started. Our eventful but satisfying day was topped off by mozzarella and ham focaccias at the bakery in Yarra Glen. And as much water as we could drink. But never have I been more grateful for a room that came with a spa bath as I bathed my aching limbs that night.

15

Green Smoothies? No Thanks!

At weekends, I get tired of the endless cycle of negative news stories on my phone and opt instead to read a real newspaper. One of my favourite columns is "My Day on a Plate" in *Sunday Life*, the *Sunday Age*'s magazine supplement. It's where notable—and some not so notable—people reveal what they eat over a day. Their diet is then analysed by a dietician who gives them non-judgmental feedback about their food choices and offers tips on how to up their intake of certain nutrients they might be lacking.

Influencers and "Wellness Gurus" who wouldn't be seen in public eating a carb-ridden sandwich often feature in the column, especially when they have a lifestyle product to flog. Their total lack of self-awareness and humourless virtue-signalling make for entertaining reading. They are so resolutely on-message, I play Wellness Guru Bingo with all their favourite buzzwords. And I can't fight off the urge to read the column while munching some delicious salted-caramel shortbread or some triple-chocolate Kāpiti ice-cream.

Along with the inevitable green smoothies made with

kale or spinach, for a Wellness Guru gold star, add bee pollen and chia seeds. Their beverage for the day has to be something lifestyle enhancing such as coconut water, or if they want to pretend they're not trying too hard, it's filtered water. Never, ever will you read, 'I drink a big gulp of tap water straight from the SodaStream bottle in the fridge as I am too lazy to find a glass.'

Then there's maca powder. Or, when they really want to lord it over their fellow Wellness Gurus, they boast about "raw activated almonds" and "raw chocolate", which is unroasted chocolate beans. Raw chocolate evangelists claim that the vitamins and minerals are preserved compared with the heated stuff.

But as one chocolate expert pointed out, if you don't heat up the beans to at least 150C, you run the risk of food poisoning such as salmonella. And what's more, it's the taste of the chocolate that should be paramount, the quality of the cacao, not whether it's raw or cooked. But try telling that to a Wellness Guru.

As for raw activated almonds, they belong in the realm of pseudo-science. And they cost twice the price of the inactive ones. Whether your nuts are active or inactive makes no difference to your health, only to your wallet, according to registered dieticians. But not content with putting almonds through their paces, another contender for Pseud of the Year boasts about "activated charcoal" in her "black detox smoothie".

Unsubstantiated claims about the health benefits of foods and supplements containing activated charcoal include reducing cholesterol, improving digestive health and removing unspecified impurities. Worryingly, charcoal, made from either coal, coconut shell, peat, wood, or even petroleum, becomes activated when you heat it with gas. Activated charcoal's only proven health benefit is when it is administered in a healthcare setting after a poisoning incident, as it binds with the poison and prevents it entering the blood stream. I don't know about you, but I don't fancy a product that's best buddies with poison in any of my drinks.

The Wellness Gurus don't get to eat their healthy treats without some form of exercise first, often the type out of reach to ordinary mortals like you and me. Mixed up with the predictable ways to exert yourself, such as running, walking and weight-training, they throw in their beautiful lifestyle for good measure. The first thing one Wellness Guru does when he wakes in the morning is make a beeline for the ocean for some paddle-boarding—a lifestyle tip difficult to replicate for most of us. Another contender for Pseud of the Year is only allowed lunch after her infrared sauna session.

Only one recent contributor, the comedian Shaun Micallef, addressed the elephant in the room: the fear of being judged by the readers. But as he makes his living by being intentionally funny, rather than unintentionally hilarious like the Wellness Gurus, he could afford to let loose with his food choices. By mid-afternoon each day, he's craving pretzels, he says, but has something less fattening instead.

The punchline is that after a very virtuous-sounding vegan dinner in the evening, he does in fact reach for the pretzels. That's about as unhealthy an entry as I've read lately, although one celebrity confessed to having not one but two glasses of wine at dinner. Then there are the virtual signallers who claim they eat dessert, when in fact it's a homemade chocolate protein ball or stewed rhubarb with apple and, wait for it, raw chocolate.

But it isn't so much about what the expert thinks or what the Wellness Gurus preach; as Shaun Micallef rightly said, it's all about what the readers will say. And they tend to speak out on social media. While the "My Day on a Plate" contributors occasionally go viral, readers are downright scathing when a green juice evangelist outlines her daily diet.

Her joyless diet consists of hot water and lemon, nuts, scrambled egg white, green tea, green juice, green salad with chia seeds, avocado and rice cakes, kale salad with more nuts, olives, dried fruit, and apple cider vinegar. Sometimes, she really pushes the boat out and treats herself to brown rice and grilled fish.

Another Guru is so satisfied with her healthy diet, she even gives out a recipe for her "natural Nutella balls", which contain cacao powder, cinnamon, coconut oil, chopped walnuts and dates, all washed down with a "homemade turmeric latte" with almond milk. The dietician refutes her claim that a few squares of raw dark chocolate have less sugar than a carrot, counselling against falling for so-called "superfoods", pointing out that the vegetable has far fewer calories than the chocolate and arguing that there is no scientific evidence supporting any health benefits to the "healthy" snacks spruiked by the guru.

Little Italy

Luckily, I am spared from this hipster food by a friend. When she comes to visit from New Zealand in March 2025, she points me in the direction of Sydney Road, Brunswick.

Brunswick is beloved of students and recent graduates as it gives out an arty vibe, is close to the University of Melbourne campus, and has great public transport with a regular tram service into the city. Sydney Road, Bruns-wick's major shopping street, boasts a highly eclectic collec-tion of shops, where you can buy, amongst other things, made-to-measure jeans and wedding gear.

I am interested in an outlet that sells the biggest range of pasta that you will find outside of Italy. From the street, the building looks like an industrial cash and carry. And the sign on the door, Mediterranean Wholesalers, indicates that it caters primarily to the restaurant and grocery trade. But according to the website, it's the largest continental food store in Australia. The size of a supermarket, it has a loyal client base who range from Italian nonnas to young families and people like me.

When I cross the threshold, I'm transported to southern Italy, circa 1980. It's like stepping into a portal of Italian daily life with decor that hasn't changed in decades. The floor is covered with cream ceramic tiles, the walls are clad in mid-brown wood and the entire place is lit by dingy strip lighting.

One side of the store sells non-food grocery items such as Italian soap powder and cleaning products. Next to those is a huge range of terracotta cooking pots and kitchen ware. I am particularly taken with the kitsch salt-shakers in a range of sizes, from small to over the top. They are all in the shape of voluptuous "chilli ladies", as I call them.

I gawp at the pasta machines, which range from the kind of appliance you'd be able to fit into a one-bedroom flat to one that makes enough pasta for a family of twelve. I once owned a pasta machine, "once" being the operative word because that's how many times I used it. But what interests me most in this place is the packaged food. Along one wall is a selection of biscuits for dunking into coffee, often consumed in Italy with an espresso for a quick breakfast either at home or at a bar on the way to work. It is going to take me at least an hour to get around this place and I really need a shot of caffeine to have the energy to do that.

The giant coffee machine in the cafe area of the vast space is going non-stop. It sits on a counter in front of which are half a dozen bistro tables covered in bright tablecloths depicting a colourful sun-drenched Italian piazza. Every table bar one is occupied. My friend nabs the seats and I queue at the counter, after taking a ticket, gawping at the freshly made cakes, cannoli and pizza by the slice. I vow to make a few return visits, just to eat my way through the menu. I get a taster of the rum baba, which has not merely a generous slug of rum in it, but appears to be saturated with it. Not wanting to get tipsy on a sweet treat, I opt for the pistachio cake instead, which is very moreish.

After coffee, I stroll around the biscuit section to the brightly coloured tins of assorted chocolates. There is, of course, the iconic Baci brand, with its silver and blue foil wrapping, but there are a dozen others I've never heard of, all teeming with hazelnuts or almonds. Then there is an entire section devoted to Italian wines and spirits. As well as classic spirits like Amaretto, Limoncello and grappa, there's Cynar, a liqueur made out of artichokes. It is as revolting as it sounds. I once bought a bottle as a joke present for BB Lookalike after a filming trip to Italy. I don't think he's ever forgiven me.

While I'm impressed with the extensive selection of wine from nearly every region in Italy, from Piedmont in the north right down to Sicily, nothing prepares me for the display of dried pasta that runs the entire length of the supermarket down two aisles. There is every pasta shape you can think of in a rainbow of colours.

If you regularly make the same old pasta dishes, this is the place to be inspired. Back in the day, I only ever paid lip service to the notion that every pasta shape is different for a reason. And I have been as guilty as the next non-Italian of subbing rigatoni with penne or tagliatelle with spaghetti. Now that I'm a big fan of Stanley Tucci's *Searching for Italy*, where the actor and author cooks his way around the country, I've come to realise the error of my ways.

On my third visit, my last before we return to the UK, a lady on the tram tells me that the place looks the same today as it did nearly 50 years ago. That explains the early 80s vibe, then. On this visit, I immerse myself in the full Italian delicatessen experience. Being as it's a Saturday morning after a public holiday when the shop was closed, the place is heaving. As I stand waiting for half an hour for my ticket number 77 to be called, I chide myself for doing this on such a busy morning. But I stay put and wait to order my "*cento grammi di prosciutto di Parma*". As every person in front of me is ordering in a weird mix of Australian-accented English and Italian, I do the same. I am pleased with myself that the person serving understands my Italian.

My order costs $6. Yes, the prosciutto is indeed $60 a kilo, but it's imported from Italy and if I bought it anywhere else in Melbourne, it may even be double that. I have little time left to indulge myself in this wonderful Italian produce before we leave Australia, so I am going to make the most of it.

16

Zen and the Art of Packing

This will be the 29th time I've moved house. I was excused from packing at my first move as I was an infant, but by the second, I was capable of tossing a few toys into a suitcase. By move 24, I had a second career: helping others relocate.

In early 2025, I start the process four months before we depart Melbourne, selling off plants and home appliances. As we won't have an employer to pick up the tab for this relocation, we need to offload everything. Our lease states that we must leave our apartment clean and unfurnished so that we can claim for the return of our rental bond. With three weeks to go until departure day, I upload photographs of our furniture to Facebook Marketplace. Then the messages start flooding in, a constant barrage of: '*Is it available? Can I grab it now?*'

It was available 30 seconds ago when I posted the ad, so why wouldn't it still be?

Irritating enquiries come in from bargain hunters who insist on making me an offer, even though I've stipulated a fixed price. For a $180 home appliance, which is cheaper by $20 than its closest rival on all the online websites, one guy offers me $100. The other chancers, without bothering to arrange to see the item, offer to "take it off my hands" for $30 less than the asking price. I can't help feeling smug when I contact the hagglers, telling them I got the full amount.

Almost as irritating are enquiries from people who don't bother to read the ad and ask where they can pick up the item. I get fed up with pointing out that I have written, in bold capital letters, that collection is from St Kilda.

I'm told to watch out for scammers who offer to pay by PayID, then a friend or relative will come and collect. The scammer "transfers" the money via phone, sending you what looks like a PayID confirmation saying the payment is pending, and they spin a story that it will take 24 hours for the payment to go through as you are a new payee. Although the confirmation looks like the real thing, if you hand over the goods, the payment disappears.

I get a message from a buyer who tells me he wants the office chair, but he can't collect as he's in bed with the 'flu.

Of course it's 'flu, you're a man, but I keep this thought to myself.

'My mum lives around the corner, so I'll send her to collect it,' he adds.

She'll be thrilled as I'm sure she has nothing better to do than run around after you.

Again, I refrain from sharing this with Bubby, as I have named this man-baby after the work experience in the Australian sitcom, *Fisk*. Sure enough, Bubby's mummy never does show up.

Worst of all, though, are the time wasters and tyre kickers. Time wasters bombard me with questions relating to the specification of the item (including serial numbers).

My response, they demand, must involve me unboxing the item, turning it upside down, photographing it from awkward angles, only to have them turn around after I've answered all their tedious questions and say that they want a different model.

Tyre kickers have too much time on their hands and too little going on in their lives. Little Miss Picky is a prime example. Her opening message is:

'Are there any marks on the chairs that I should know about before I come?'

Tyre kicker alert. *'Any imperfections should be visible in the photographs, which you can magnify. They are used chairs and are priced accordingly,'* I write back.

She arranges to come on Wednesday night, ghosts me when I confirm, then contacts me the next day to ask if she can come the following night.

'It will be after 5.30pm,' she tells me.

'Fine,' I write, giving her the address. *'I'll be in an online class, but ring the bell and BB Lookalike will let you in. If you want them, you can pay him.'*

As I relax into my Pilates class the next evening, I get the feeling something is off. She'll either be a no-show or won't buy the chairs. At 6pm, she messages me that she won't get here for another half an hour.

'Will that be alright?'

I reply yes, even though I mean no, then grab a glass of wine while preparing dinner. She arrives at 6.30pm, takes one look at the chairs and gushes that she likes them. She sits in both, declaring them more comfortable than they look.

'I'll take them,' she says. The next moment, she jumps out of the chair like she's been stung by a wasp, stares intently at it and spots something that displeases her. Obviously, there must be a mark that I didn't tell her about, before I dragged her all the way over to St Kilda.

'It's so difficult when you buy second-hand,' she complains.

It's not that difficult when you're getting these for a song. If you want perfection, you'll be paying three times the price, I think.

'I'll have to think about it,' she says.

'I've got loads of interest,' I tell her, which is an exaggeration. 'You'll need to make up your mind now.'

'All good,' the entitled one says, beating a hasty retreat. After our delayed dinner, I contact the six other buyers who have expressed interest, but they've all fallen away.

We know a buyer means business when he has not only organised a Man With a Van, but wants, in addition to the replica Eames office chair, the desk, which is solid beech with drawers and a handy stand for a printer.

'I'm in the middle of writing my PhD,' he tells us, as he eyes up BB Lookalike's books.

'They're coming with me,' BB Lookalike cuts the student off at the pass, before he can enquire about those too. I'm not sentimental about any of the furniture we bought, but I'm glad the chair and the desk are going to someone who will appreciate them, rather than a dealer who just wants to make money out of them.

'I've just moved house,' the student adds.

'Is there anything else you need?'

'I'll take the blue rug.'

'For $20, it's yours.'

He walks out of the apartment with the rug under his arm and a list of everything else we are giving away. When he later sends us a photo of his new office set up with the desk and the chair in pride of place, I get a buzz from that. The chair, the desk and the office were crucial to our survival during all three Covid lockdowns, when BB Lookalike worked from home, carrying out lectures on Zoom and meetings on Teams.

'*I'm glad they went to a good home,*' I text.

'*I'll take the kettle, the toaster and the vacuum cleaner,*' he writes back. As these are essential items we'll need right up until we leave, we arrange a pick-up on moving day, before the professional carpet cleaner comes in. For all the other items that aren't worth anything, I load up the "granny tractor", aka the shopping trolley, ready to take them to the nearest charity shop. I give away linen, crockery, books and towels, as I'd far rather they went to charity rather than landfill.

A friend thinks charity shops are getting pickier, as she's watched volunteers throwing books into landfill when they think no one is looking. And she could be right. One Sunday, I come unstuck when I encounter a snotty woman in the Sacred Heart op shop.

'We only take items that we can sell,' she says, eyeing up the bakeware as though I've brought her a dish of fried rat to try. 'And the items must be clean.'

What a cheek, I think. 'They've all been through the dishwasher,' I tell her.

'And we don't take non-matching crockery,' she adds.

That's shifting the goalposts.

All my non-matching crockery was bought from an op shop, but evidently not from this one. I take back my offending bakeware and quietly trot off to the Salvation Army shop, which is a bit of a schlep to Balaklava, but worth it for the big grin and thank you I get.

Salvation Army Volunteer one, Sacred Heart Volunteer nil.

As our departure date gets ever closer, I'm too busy to do the charity shop run. I leave a couple of items in the communal reception area on the ground floor of our building. Another tenant must have recently moved out as a saucepan has been dumped there for over 24 hours.

Our stuff is nicer than that, I tell myself, leaving my tired-looking orchid out first thing in the morning. By lunchtime it's gone.

As I'm desperate to get rid of more of the mismatched crockery and glassware the snotty volunteer turned her nose up at, I pack them into a box, ready for the St Kilda Esplanade Sunday Market. The traders all have vans, so if there is something someone wants, they can help themselves. The traders arrive at 7am. By 3pm, everything in the box has been picked up.

In A Spin

Two weeks before we move, I advertise the washer/dryer for $180, $20 cheaper than its nearest competitor. I have 514 clicks on my listing, indicating that it's popular. A buyer is so keen he turns up the same day with cash.

Deal done. But now I'm faced with paying to wash every load of laundry at the laundrette. The cheapest one I can find, at $5 a wash, is also the nearest. It's forty years since I last set foot in a launderette and back then, the machines were coin-operated, which meant that I had to have the right combination of pound coins and loose change. Coins are still accepted, but now there's a far more convenient Pay by Smartphone option, where I scan a QR code. But I pay a 25c surcharge on top of the $5 wash or the $5 dry.

The one thing that hasn't changed is how warm and cosy a laundrette can be on a cold winter's day, so I quite enjoy washing day. By my second visit, I've mastered the art of loading up the granny tractor, separating out the hot wash items from the cold ones, and placing them into two machines.

The timer reads 30 minutes, giving me just enough time to nip over the road to Woodfrog Bakery for a take-away skinny flat white coffee.

'You look nice,' the barista says. I look down at my grey joggers and matching coat.

'It's my "going to the launderette" outfit,' I tell him, flattered at the compliment.

Who knew doing laundry could be so sociable?

I slip back into the launderette. Seated next to the door is a pasty-looking young woman with mousy hair plastered to her head. She is coughing.

I don't like the sound of that.

Edging past her, I sit 2 metres away, facing the dryers. I have precisely 17 minutes left on my wash and pull out my laptop to start writing.

Engrossed in my work, I am startled when an insouciant young miss sits down two seats away from me and shoves the strap from my backpack over to my side.

'I'm sorry,' I say. She regards me with indifference, then ignores me. I don't know what's triggered her, but something evidently has as she can't sit still for more than 30 seconds. She gets up, hurtling from one side of the launderette to the other.

Maybe she's on something.

I call this part of St Kilda "Drug Dealers' Corner" as it's close to the needle exchange. But whatever has upset her, I am clearly in her way, and what's more, the two washing machines I'm using are next to hers. She flings open her door, which crashes across one of my machines so I can't remove my washing. She gathers all her washing in a random bundle and shoves it under her arm, while I methodically fold the clothes from the machine I can access into neat piles. This seems to make Little Miss Angry angrier still.

I watch her as she slams her way out of the laundrette and stomps off up the hill. I will *not* be having some of whatever she's on!

17

Goodbye City Life

In the last few frenetic weeks before we leave, I make it my mission to consume, give away or dispose of all the opened jars and packets left in our pantry. I feel guilty when I throw food out that is still in date. And I get a perverse thrill out of finding ways to use up ingredients, like my very own *MasterChef* Mystery Box Challenge.

But there are some foods that even I'm struggling with, namely lime marmalade and anchovies. Believe it or not, I do manage to find recipes for each of them, although if I'm honest, the anchovies are going to be a lot easier to use up than the lime marmalade. There are only so many bread-and-butter puddings I can make in the next three weeks. (And I end up making none.)

The anchovy challenge is solved by a recipe for the French version of pizza, Pissaladière, in Australian chef Shannon Bennett's *28 Days in Provence*. This requires a whopping 16 of the little blighters. (Before you say it, yes, that is a lot of salt, probably my quota for the year). And that's not counting the 20 Niçoise olives that are included in the dish. If there is a next time I make it, I will be halving the salty elements.

As for the marmalade, that becomes a substitute for Rose's Lime Juice in a recipe for Tequila and Sweet Lime Mayo. And, you guessed it, I also have leftover tequila. Both ingredients are measured in teaspoons, so I still have a long way to go. If it was summer, I'd turn the tequila into a couple of Margaritas, but with a top temperature in the teens as we head into winter in Australia, it's not really the weather for it.

<hr>

So Long, Faulty Towers

Sunday 15 June is our last morning waking up at Faulty Towers. I'm out of bed before the 5.30am alarm call of the sadistic Sunday morning street cleaners' truck. While I wait for the tea to brew, for old time's sake, I can't resist opening the curtains and peering down at the truck as it does wheelies around the Palais Theatre carpark.

I watch a second street sweeper make its way along the Esplanade, scrubbing away the debris of another Saturday night in St Kilda. Like a cross between a giant vacuum cleaner and a carwash, the vehicle scoops up everything in its path, including the torrent of insults hurled from every householder who has the misfortune to have a bedroom facing onto the street. Whoever the neat freak is behind the pre-dawn clean-up, they don't give a damn about the ratepayers who might want a Sunday morning sleep-in.

We cook a celebratory breakfast out of the remaining leftovers in the fridge and reminisce about the good times we've had here. It's a busy day ahead with three sets of buyers and family coming around to collect the bed, the fridge, sofa, TV and standard lamp. And on top of that, we're checking into our temporary digs, where we'll be staying for the next five nights.

We were planning on staying around the corner, at the Paris end of Acland Street in a serviced apartment. I didn't pay too much attention to the size of it when I booked it online. But as it was so close, I decided to check it out in person.

It's just as well I did. The one-bedroom apartment, perfect for a minimalist, certainly wasn't going to fit our four large suitcases. I cancelled that and, for not much more rent, found a similar-sized apartment to Faulty Towers in a modern block on Fitzroy Street, close to a small supermarket, a French bakery and a bistro. Although we're still eating our way through our leftover groceries, if we don't fancy cooking for the rest of the week, in addition to the bistro, there's a renovated Irish pub, The Fifth Province. I've been looking for an excuse to go to The Fifth for ages. The only downside of the arrangement is that for the next five nights, we will be paying rent on two places, which can't be helped.

By 3pm, all the furniture has been collected and it's time to move on to our temporary digs, 188 Fitzroy Street. It is somewhere I must have walked past umpteen times, but never so much as bothered to glance up, as from the outside it looks like every other modern apartment block in Melbourne.

BB Lookalike and I read the instructions in the confirmation email and collect the keys from a local restaurant. The keys come with a fob which opens not one but two sets of glass doors into the building. To our right when we enter, seated behind a desk, is a concierge, no less.

Once past the concierge, we wait for the lifts. Yes, lifts plural. Three in fact. What luxury. The lifts don't work without the key fob, and so I wave ours at the sensor before pressing the button for our floor.

We follow the instructions to get to our apartment and turn the key in the lock. It is a haven of calm and comfort, with impressively thick double-glazing that shuts out most of the noise on Fitzroy Street. The second bedroom, we allocate as the packing room, parking our four suitcases there. There is a spacious balcony with a table and four chairs, which we admire from behind a thick wall of glass as it's far too cold to venture out.

We have a full oven and four-burner hob, which will be useful for rustling up a cooked breakfast, even if we aren't planning on cooking much at night. Sunday night, we have leftover seafood pasta, and on Monday and Tuesday, cassoulet from a jar which I bought from a French cafe in South Yarra. A salad and baguette jazz up what is essentially a Gallic riff on sausages and beans.

The building is so quiet that we have a blissful night's sleep. The bed is super comfortable and this place turns out to be the perfect escape for our last hectic days in Melbourne. However, we're not content with staying put. Our curiosity gets the better of us and we want to investigate the rooftop area.

There is only one lift to get us there, again accessible with a key fob. Once we step out of the lift, we are dumbstruck by the 360-degree panorama. To the southwest, we can even see Faulty Towers as well as the beach beyond. Looking north, we admire Albert Park Lake stretched out below us.

I bet they make a killing here over Grand Prix weekend, I think.

But the most stunning sight is from the poolside sun loungers, over the infinity pool towards Port Phillip Bay. There are two barbecues on the rooftop, but as it's midwinter, even we aren't tempted. When we come back to

Melbourne, I hope we get the chance to stay in this building again. We started this new adventure five-and-a-half years ago on grungy St Kilda Road, then we graduated to Faulty Towers. But we've hit the heights with this one, halfway between the two buildings.

On Monday, we begin the final countdown. We start with the packers who will uplift all of BB Lookalike's workbooks from the University of Melbourne, drive to St Kilda and pack all the books in the home office along with our clothes, a couple of small appliances and lightweight furniture. On Tuesday, we need to have a last-minute clean out, ready for the apartment and carpet cleaning on Wednesday and Thursday.

The office and two bedrooms in the Faulty Towers apartment are carpeted, but since the heavy furniture has been removed, there are noticeable dents in the carpet pile. Worried that the Agent will withhold some of the bond, I google various solutions. On Wednesday, the cleaner suggests putting a damp cloth on the dents and then applying a hot iron, which should bring up the pile. She offers to iron the carpets while I trade jobs with her and volunteer to clean the oven. It's a job I hate, but I'm on a mission to get 100% of our bond back.

We spend Wednesday and Thursday making the place spick and span. By 2pm on the Thursday, BB Lookalike and I are ready to catch a tram to the Real Estate Agent's office to drop the keys off. It's a good feeling. All we can do is keep our fingers crossed and hope we've done enough to pass the final agency inspection. Our lease doesn't end officially until 24 June, but we have a train to catch on Friday the 20th, which is why we're vacating a few days early.

It's a relief to be staying away from the chaos of the move, although we've had to pack our two suitcases with enough clothes for two weeks, catering for three different seasons: winter clothes for Melbourne and Adelaide, lighter layers for Alice Springs, summer clothes and swimmers for Darwin and Singapore. It's always shoes (appropriately) that trip me up for sartorial challenges like this. My best tip is to pack the others and wear your heaviest shoes/boots to travel, although I don't fancy that for the last leg, the 14-hour-plus marathon from Singapore to London.

The Fifth Province

The Fifth has been on our radar for the past five-and-a-half years, but since the pub was refurbished in 2023, introducing not only a dress code (smart casual) for indoors but a champagne bar to boot, I've been keen to try it. Irish food and drink don't work with hot weather, but now that it's winter, and the pub is just on our doorstep, it's looking like a tempting night out.

The menu features all the big hits of Irish food, from boiled bacon and cabbage with parsley sauce, to a beef and Guinness stew with champ. I am torn between the cider steamed mussels with chorizo, smoked paprika, Irish butter and soda bread versus fish and chips. The latter win out. Unlike most places in Australia, the chips are properly crispy and not flabby and anaemic looking.

As it's a school night, we only admire the spirits menu, with its impressive list of both Scottish and Irish single malt whisky/whiskey (spelt with the addition of an e in Ireland).

Goodbye, City Life

Most of my travels have involved getting from A to B in the shortest time possible. Until we moved back to Australia in

2020, I had rarely even had a stopover on the flight from London. It was only after my food poisoning episode in 2022 that it dawned on me that it was no good arriving at my destination feeling so exhausted, I couldn't function for the next week, just for the sake of saving 24 hours. I may live by the mantra that while you can always make more money, you can never get more time, but I'm now in a position where I do have more time to make the journey part of the experience.

And it's high time we saw the interior of Australia from ground level, rather than from the air. Our farewell to city life coincides with a milestone anniversary, and being married for 25 years deserves to be celebrated in style. And what could be better than taking a luxury train from the bottom to the top of Australia?

The iconic Ghan runs between Adelaide and Darwin via Alice Springs. But before we catch it, we need to find a way of getting to Adelaide. I research the flights from Melbourne and compare them with the Overland train service. While a budget airline will get us there for a reduced price, what it won't do is put up with the mountain of luggage that we have between us. Despite jettisoning clothes at the last minute, I have 21.5kg in one bag and 16.5kg in the other, as well as hand luggage.

By the time I've compared like-for-like services, the train works out to be cheaper, even in Premium Economy. There's a generous luggage allowance (2 x 30kg bags plus 10kg hand luggage) and we get breakfast, lunch and afternoon tea thrown in for the same price as a peak-time airfare. Plus, we get to ride on not one, but two long-distance trains across Australia, with the chance to see both scenery and wildlife at ground level.

We leave St Kilda for the last time at first light on Friday 20 June 2025. A cab takes us along Canterbury

Road, past Middle Park and Albert Park, where we've eaten, shopped and walked these past five-and-a-half years. It's a quick 15-minute ride to Southern Cross Station and we're there by 7.15am.

The Overland offers a full old-fashioned customer service experience, evident from the warm welcome we get at Platform 2 from the check-in staff of Journey Beyond, the company running the trip. It's such a contrast with the airlines. There's no self-service kiosk, where you must print out your own luggage tags. Neither is there a bag drop. We make our way to the Luggage Hall where we check in all our luggage under 20kg with a staff member. We'll take the one 21.5kg bag on the train with us. Although our train doesn't leave until 8.05am, we are encouraged to board early, as the manager doesn't want her passengers shivering on the platform.

Our Red Premium train carriage seating is in comfy reclining armchairs in a 1–2 configuration with a spacious aisle between the three seats. There's enough legroom for even the loftiest of the Harlem Globetrotters. Between the Standard Class and Red Premium carriages is a licensed cafe with big picture windows, where we can enjoy a decent coffee and spectacular views.

The Overland train stretches for 189 metres and has seven carriages, each one able to carry 36 passengers. Although it feels epic taking a train for a 11-hour journey, there is none of the same drama as there is leaving by plane. Unless you're a trainspotter, watching trains depart doesn't have the buzz of looking at planes taking off and landing. Nor is there any of the excitement of taxiing out to the runway then waiting in the queue. Then, my favourite bit, when the plane rattles and shakes as it rumbles down the runway, gathering speed. There's that moment when you sit back in your seat, willing the aircraft to go up, up and away. Alas, we slip out of Melbourne for the last time without fanfare, gliding through the industrial western suburbs, past desolate-looking factories and warehouses more suited for crime movies than a poignant goodbye.

Wonderful Adelaide

At Dimboola, a railway town and the informal halfway point between Melbourne and Adelaide, the drivers do a change over. Our train is held up as our new driver is randomly breath tested. After a lunch of spinach quesadillas and salad, accompanied by 200ml of sparkling chardonnay pinot noir, I'm relieved it's not the passengers being breathalysed.

And then, we're off again. We cross the border into South Australia. The only reason I know we've done that is we pass through Bordertown—it doesn't take much imagination to work out how it got to be called that. It would be fair to say there isn't a lot going on here for visitors, unless you're desperate to see the birthplace of Bob Hawke, Australia's 23rd Prime Minister.

To give Bob his due, his humble beginnings didn't stop him from becoming the "people's PM", a job he held for a record eight years. And my claim to fame is that BB Lookalike and I once shared a lift with him inside the Sydney Opera House, for an Opera Australia performance of *Romeo and Juliet*.

As the train rolls onwards towards Adelaide in the late afternoon, we spot the mighty Murray River at Murray Bridge. I know the town for its fresh produce, especially tomatoes, which I buy from the farmers' markets. But Murray Bridge is better known as a tourist destination for river cruises. We pass it at the perfect time of day, as the sun sets and lights up the river boats parked next to the bridge.

The train is running half an hour late, and at dusk, we pass through the Adelaide Hills, which are wilder and more remote than I was expecting. At 6.30pm, we arrive into Adelaide Parkland Station in the suburbs.

The baggage collection is chaotic, as all our bags are dumped in one large pile. Passengers climb over each other to retrieve their belongings, and then dash to the long queue waiting for taxis. With our four bags plus hand luggage, we are shoved to the back of the line. Luckily, one of the Journey Beyond staff assists us in getting a taxi, as some of the drivers take one look at our excess luggage and move onto the next passenger in line.

Our hotel, or rather apart-hotel, is on North Terrace, and we've been upgraded to a two-bedroom. It comes with a kitchen the size of ours in St Kilda.

By the time we're ready to go and find dinner, it's 7.45pm. Acting on a recommendation from the hotel manager, we weave our way between girls on a night out and guys on a works' do to The Little Hunter, a steak restaurant just around the corner.

'I don't fancy our chances at getting a table,' I say to BB Lookalike, looking around at the crowds. 'It seems fully booked to me.' But after consultation with her colleagues, a waiter shows us to the table right by the door. We only have an hour and a half before our table is turned, so we promise to order quickly. We mumble our appreciation.

I order gnocchi with ragout sauce and BB Lookalike chooses the roast chicken. The wine list is extensive, and what's more, all of it comes from South Australia. We start with a celebratory prosecco from Mount Barker and follow it with a shiraz that has the delightful name of Down the

Rabbit Hole, from McLaren Vale. We're now officially in holiday mode, after all!

It's been fifteen years since I last visited Adelaide and I can't believe the transformation. My first impression back then was that it was a conservative city that lacked the energy of Melbourne. Today, I stand corrected. This part of town is abuzz with life and revellers enjoying themselves.

I find out the next day, thanks to a friend who gives up her day off to drive me around, that Adelaide has it all. There are fabulous beaches and vineyards, all within thirty minutes of the city, and the restaurants are world class. I'm so glad I came back.

18

The Red Centre

On Sunday morning, we're out the door at seven. Unless we get a walk in now, we won't have any proper exercise until we reach Darwin on the other side of Australia. And being the restless soul that I am, I need to keep up my daily step count.

Our walk takes us past Government House, built in the Regency style in 1840, situated in park-like grounds. Although there have been additions made to it, through the railings, we glimpse the cream-coloured stone and shuttered windows of the original house. We pass the University of Adelaide's historic stone buildings, also 19th century, on our way to the Botanical Gardens.

But the gardens are shut, so we turn around, taking a short cut across Botanic Park where hundreds of grey-headed flying foxes, or fruit bats, hang upside down from the trees. All I can think about is not walking underneath them as the last thing we need is to be showered with bat poo.

We escape unscathed.

As we walk back to the hotel, I think about Adelaide

and South Australia. They're Australia's hidden gems. So many international tourists flock to Sydney and Uluru, but miss out this beautiful part of the country.

We grab coffee and an almond croissant at a cafe near the hotel, and then I spend a frantic half hour repacking. There is only room for hand luggage on the train because space is at a premium and all our other bags must go in the luggage car. If I forget something, it's too bad. We won't see our luggage again until we reach Darwin.

___

Setting Off on the Ghan

We arrive at the Ghan terminal two hours before departure time, as instructed. We have to check out of our Adelaide hotel by 10am, so this is as good a place as any to hang around in.

The terminal is packed and there are long queues for check-in. Once we have parted company with our hold luggage, we are offered a celebration drink of sparkling wine, Buck's Fizz or orange juice. As it's only 11, we compromise with a Buck's Fizz.

At 11.30am, we are allowed to board. We walk down the platform to carriage B where we are greeted by a smiley on-board attendant, who directs us to our forward-facing compartment, which is as I'd requested. The room is set up with a three-seater sofa and cushions, and a generous-sized side table. The "premium" element of the room is the en suite bathroom, a real luxury compared with the overnight train I took from Florence to Munich in my 20s. I was in a shared carriage of four and we all had to sleep sitting upright. The bathroom was down the corridor and it certainly didn't run to a shower. Yet being young, I had no trouble sleeping. In fact, it was difficult to wake me up.

I wonder how I'll sleep on this one.

On this train, not only is there a shower and a loo in a room the size of a cupboard, but it's been designed as a "wet room", using an ingenious shower curtain to create a temporary partition for the sink and the loo. I can't wait to try it out.

As this is going to be home for the next 55 hours, the first thing I do is unpack. There's a tiny wardrobe with four hangers and I hang up all the clothes I brought in my carry-on luggage. Underneath the wardrobe is a square cupboard, just large enough to store a backpack.

Inside the bathroom is a tiny vanity unit, but it's enough to store a small make-up bag. I was gifted a hanging sponge bag in which I have fitted all the essentials I'll need for the trip.

Once the unpacking is done, I stash my carry-on bag on the shelf above the wardrobe and bathroom door. It's so high I need to stand on the sofa, but I can just about reach it.

Our guest services manager drops by and delivers our mealtime schedule. First up is a two-course lunch at 1pm. I have one glass of wine as I'm pacing myself for tonight's dinner, as I'm going to need something to knock me out to be able to sleep on board. It dawns on me that's why I slept so well on that European train all those years ago—a fellow backpacker brought out a bottle of something which we took turns drinking, and I know for a fact that it was far stronger than wine.

We spend the afternoon staring out the window, looking at the scenery—bush-covered hills and tawny grasslands—pass by. At Port Augusta, we watch the setting sun from the train. We are slotted in for an early dinner at 6.30pm, but we head up to the bar first for an aperitif. It's a jolly atmosphere in there, as the party people have been propping up the bar since 5pm.

The restaurant manager calls us to our table, which seats four, so she ushers in another couple to dine with us. It reminds me of old-fashioned passengers ships, which had two meal sittings and passengers sharing tables. Our dining companions are a nurse and a businessman from South Australia, who we met in the bar. It hadn't occurred to me as we chatted over drinks that we'd be sharing a table with them, but luckily, we are all from a generation that learnt social skills. We sound each other out, careful to avoid any controversial subjects like politics.

The couple exude good humour and bonhomie, so after starting off with safe topics, including why we chose this trip and means of travel, we feel comfortable enough to venture into subjects that include the mushroom murder trial gripping the nation, where a woman served deadly poisonous mushrooms, she claims mistakenly, to her family, as well as the daft conspiracy theories that we came across during lockdown. It helps the conversation to flow as the evening wears on that our three courses, showcasing local ingredients, are accompanied some of South Australia's very drinkable wines.

After our sumptuous dinner, rather than retire to the bar, BB Lookalike and I return to our carriage to find the sitting area has been converted into two bunk beds, with a step ladder up to the top bunk. It takes a bit of practice to manoeuvre around each other in the tiny space, but we manage to arrange ourselves like parcels and pack ourselves away into our bunks, with me on the ground floor and BB Lookalike upstairs.

I had thought that I might get claustrophobia, sleeping in such a confined space. But the experience reminds me of being eight years old, on the aforementioned passenger ship, which took us all the way from Tilbury Docks in Essex to Wellington, New Zealand. We were in a shared cabin, Mum, my sister and me, with a single lady who ended up being assigned to a cabin with a family. That journey lasted a month, so I reckon I'll cope with two-and-a-half days. It helps that the temperature on the train is a constant 22C, and although that is a little warmer than I would like at night, with the assistance of ear plugs and an eye mask, I manage to get to sleep without any problem at all.

The Outback

As I drift in and out of consciousness the following morning, I compare our trip with Agatha Christie's *Murder on the Orient Express*. I console myself that it's highly unlikely that an avalanche is going to derail our train, but what would happen if a very large kangaroo leapt across our path? It's an occupational hazard of being a train driver in Australia. In Victoria, there are around 60 kangaroo collisions per month. One hotspot, Kangaroo Flat (it would be called that, wouldn't it) on the Bendigo Line, is notorious.

As well as avoiding kangaroos, and avalanches, I fervently hope that we don't have a killer on board and have to call upon the services of Hercule Poirot. It would take Hercule too long to get here, so we'd have to settle for a local detective. And if someone does get themselves murdered, where will they store the body? Will they shove the poor person in a seat covered in blankets until we get to Alice Springs, like they do on an aircraft when someone dies?

It's early days, but none of our fellow passengers seem capable of wielding anything more than a knife and fork.

BB Lookalike and I took a good look at them when we boarded, so maybe we could become amateur sleuths if the worst does happen. One couple did stand out from the happy crowd when we were waiting to be called to our table for dinner last night as they rudely told the dining car manager that they didn't want to sit with anyone and insisted on a table to themselves. Younger than most of their fellow passengers on this train, they then spent their evening ignoring each other and playing with their phones. As we have no internet or cell coverage, I'm intrigued as to what they were doing on them.

It's 6am on Monday, and as the train slows down, I pull up the window shade. It's not yet light, but the sky is full of stars. I rearrange the bed covers and move my pillows so that I'm facing the window.

'Those stars are incredible,' I say. BB Lookalike gets down off his top bunk just as there's a knock on the door. I jump up, throwing my dressing gown around me. It's Anthony, our carriage attendant, with the two cups of tea we ordered the night before.

'Good morning, we're at Marla,' he tells us. I thank him, grateful for the tea. The northbound Ghan stops at Marla on Mondays and Fridays for 45 minutes to allow passengers to experience an Outback sunrise. It's something I've always wanted to do, but this is my first opportunity. I can't wait.

'I'll let you know when you can get off the train,' he adds.

As the train comes to a complete stop, I jump into the shower.

You haven't lived until you can say you've showered on a train, I think, but I reckon I'd get more brownie points if I did it while we were moving.

Marla (population 70) became an official government

town in May 1981 during the construction of the Stuart Highway. This tar-sealed road is the vital artery that connects Adelaide and Darwin. Marla is 160km south of the Northern Territory border and has a roadhouse, 24-hour fuel, accommodation, camping, a hotel, general store, and restaurant. Only we don't see any of that as the railway line is south of the Stuart Highway and from our train window, it looks like we're in Nowheresville.

As we wait to get off the train, I do a quick calculation that we've been travelling for 18 hours and we're still in South Australia. And although I have to look this up on our route map, the distance we've covered so far is 1,000km.

This is one huge country.

Because there's no station here in the Outback that would accommodate a train a kilometre long (when all 36 carriages are included), our stop is a railway siding. To get us on and off the train, the staff bring out a set of portable steps for each carriage. I'm dressed in hiking trousers, a long-sleeved top and a leather jacket as the night-time temperature in the Outback at the coolest time of the year is a chilly 12C. All the other passengers are sensibly dressed for the conditions, apart from one couple who are wearing Ghan-issued dressing gowns.

They must be in Platinum Class.

Instead of tea and coffee, they lord it over the rest of us, sipping champagne out of paper cups.

Rather them than me at this time of day.

I'm making the most of the opportunity to walk in the cool morning air. If you've ever been to the desert, you'll appreciate the contrast between surprisingly cool mornings and skyrocketing temperatures for the rest of the day. I'm grateful for the coffee, but pass on the bacon and egg roll. Brunch is being served from 10am and if it's anything like as good as last night's dinner, I'm saving myself for that.

The land is pancake flat, so our view across to the eastern sky is uninterrupted. Venus shines brightly, high in the violet-coloured darkness. As we look towards the horizon, the colours change to lavender and pale orange. And then the sun's dazzling rays burst out in every direction. I try not to look at it directly, but I sneak a peek at the orange sunburst, lighting up the desert landscape as though it was on fire.

By 7.30am, the light show is over and we are on our way again. Day 2 of our journey promises to be action packed. Barely have we finished brunch than we are getting ready for our afternoon's excursion in Alice Springs. Tourism is a mainstay of the area as it's touted as the gateway to Uluru (although Uluru is still a few hours' drive away and not on our itinerary this time).

"The Alice", as it's known to Australians, is a town that makes headlines, often for all the wrong reasons. When I mentioned to a social media contact that I was going, she advised me to be careful about walking around the town with valuables. As a response to violent crime, the state government has lowered the age of criminal responsibility to ten years old. This may be the same as the other states and territories in Australia, but here in Alice Springs, children are locked up four times more often than anywhere else in the country. One day, these kids will leave prison, and if there has been no effort put into giving them skills for meaningful work, then all they will do is re-offend.

Violent crime statistics aside, I'm keen to see the place for myself. Outside the train station, coaches are lining up to take us Ghan passengers on our different excursions. BB Lookalike and I have chosen a combined cultural and botanical tour through Simpsons Gap, known as

Rungutjirpa to the traditional owners, the Arrernte People. Our tour guide, Miguel, moved from Spain to Alice Springs for the chance to show off the area to tourists. He's joined by Jared, a registered Arrernte guide.

Our first stop is at a walking trail to view Ghost Gums, a species of eucalyptus with striking silver-coloured bark. We're told to stay on the path and watch out for snakes. I packed trail shoes and hiking trousers for the off-train excursions as a precaution and am in my go-to long-sleeved sun-protection shirt, as well as a hat and sunglasses. We are very lucky with the heat as this is winter in the Northern Territory, with the maximum temperature today reaching a manageable 25C. And what's more, there aren't too many flies bothering us.

After admiring the view of the West MacDonnell Ranges, we're back on the bus to Simpsons Gap. The Gap, located about 20km west of Alice Springs, is on the Larapinta Trail, a walk of close to 230km that runs along the spine of the West MacDonnell Ranges, or Tjoritja to give them the Arrernte name. Between the two sides of the ranges is Roe Creek, which is rich with flora and fauna, including the black-footed rock wallaby. These creatures are hard to see as their markings are identical to the rocks, but I manage to spot one as it hops away. I'm surprised at how small and agile it is, but then it would need to be as the terrain is steep.

As well as being a trove of information about the landscape, Jared demonstrates how to find water in the desert. He moves on to explain his people's creation story, known as the Dreamtime, as well as the complex kinship systems that they evolved, which have enabled them to inhabit this land successfully for over 60,000 years. On the bus back to the train, all I can think about is that's 20,000 years longer than modern humans have occupied Britain.

So much for the narrow definition of what a sophisticated society is.

Miguel adds a bonus stop, which wasn't on our itinerary: a trip up ANZAC Hill, 608m above sea level. It's a memorial to the soldiers who fought in overseas wars from WW1 onwards, as well as the highest spot in town to watch sunrise or sunset. We catch the afternoon sun's golden rays illuminating the surrounding mountains.

After our sightseeing, we return to Alice Springs to catch the train for the last leg of our journey up to Darwin. It's been a long day so I'm looking forward to sitting down for our final dinner on the train. Three courses on consecutive evenings is quite the indulgence, so imagine what it must be like on a cruise ship! I'd have to either pace myself or spend my days doing laps around the deck and in the gym.

Our dining companions tonight are a farming couple from New Zealand's South Island, on the Ghan to celebrate a milestone birthday. They listen politely as we tell them stories of our stay on a high-country sheep station in Mackenzie Country and how much we miss New Zealand.

I hope we don't bore them too much.

Salties and Freshies

I don't sleep so well on the second night as I'm woken by the motion of the train. I drift off again and I wake up to the realisation that tonight, I will be sleeping in a room that doesn't move. Or at least, I hope it doesn't. Darwin doesn't have earthquakes, does it?

Breakfast, which consists of two courses, fresh juice and fruit with yoghurt followed by poached eggs with smoked salmon, is another triumph. How I wish I could visit the on-board kitchens where the chefs produce these gourmet meals, but I doubt they'd appreciate me gawping at them as they serve so many customers.

As our train approaches the town of Katherine, I recall a previous river cruise when we were last up in the Northern Territory, on the mis-named Alligator River. Captain Philip Parker King, a 19th century explorer, has been confusing tourists in the region since 1820 as he mistakenly identified the reptiles found there as alligators, not the crocodiles they actually are.

Our excursion today is to see Nitmiluk Rock Art on the Katherine River. Anthony, our carriage attendant, gave us a handy tip when he recommended the Nitmiluk Gorge cruise as it covers the same ground as the dedicated rock art one, only it's longer.

Like at Marla, we passengers get on and off the train via the portable steps. BB Lookalike and I are herded onto our coach, and after a twenty-minute drive, we arrive at the dock where the cruise boats depart from. Nitmiluk National Park and the cruises are run by the traditional owners of this area, the Jawoyn.

Our boat captain Jodi runs the tour single-handedly and does a brilliant job multi-tasking as our guide. She has a passion for showing tourists the river and its gorges, as well as sharing the creation myth of how the gorges were created. It's a rainbow serpent story, with each of the 13 gorges a different part of the snake.

As we glide along the jungle-green waters of the first gorge, our insignificance within this landscape is amplified by the majestic sandstone cliffs surrounding us on both sides. At the end of the first gorge, Jodi pulls up, allowing us to disembark to view the two rock art sites. The paintings, in vivid red ochre or iron oxide, have been dated to at least 10,000 years ago and realistically depict food sources such as fish, meat and turtle eggs. But the stand-out for me is the mythological rainbow serpent, or Bolung as he's known around here. He's huge and not the kind of creature I'd like to encounter with his enormous thrashing tail, not unlike the real creatures that inhabit this gorge. Yes, you guessed it—crocodiles.

Even though the Katherine River and its gorges are fresh water, the giant salt-water crocodile now calls the river system home, along with its littler and more benign fresh-water cousin. And that's why, no matter how tempting the water might look on a scorching hot day in summer, swimming is forbidden.

We spot three fresh-water crocodiles, all juveniles, sunning themselves on rocks. I'm surprised at how small they are and I can see why they fall prey to the salties. Better them than some hapless swimmer who ignored the warnings, I guess.

Along the river, Jodi points out the saltwater crocodile traps. The most dangerous time of year for salties is after the wet season when Nitmiluk Gorge is monitored not just by rangers on the ground, but from the air by helicopter. As water levels drop, saltwater crocodiles that become trapped and can't swim out are removed. They are sedated while they're in the traps, but I pity the poor vet who has to give an 18-foot-long bad-tempered reptile a shot of Valium to calm it down.

That's one job I wouldn't fancy.

I'm so immersed in this side trip that for a while, I forget that we are on a long-distance train journey. But all too soon, we are being bused back to the Ghan for one last time. The antisocial couple who refused to sit with anyone at dinner are on our bus, although I never noticed them on the cruise. They have somehow found a network connection and are busy bellowing at a family member. I am brought back down to earth with a bump.

We are served our final two-course lunch. Our dining companions are a teacher and a retired engineer from Victoria, who are continuing their journey on a small-ship cruise to Western Australia, a trip I hope to do some day. BB Lookalike and I spend the rest of the afternoon staring at the scenery as we make our way towards Darwin, our final stop. Noticing that the Travel Scrabble that went into our on-board luggage is untouched, I'm glad that my assumption there wouldn't be enough to keep us occupied on our journey was wrong.

Did this trip deliver everything I hoped for? No, it surpassed it. I wanted to experience the real Australia, without having to hire a 4WD vehicle, a satellite phone and all the other paraphernalia you need to drive across the vast deserts of the Outback. Sure, we were cosseted along the way, but nothing beats seeing the world pass by at ground level at an average speed of 85km/53mph. Travel for me now isn't just about the destination, but savouring every moment of the journey.

19

Homeward Bound

We arrive in Darwin at 5.30pm. Luggage collection here is seamless, in contrast to the chaos on arrival in Adelaide after our trip on the Overland. Why Journey Beyond can't put the same infrastructure in place for both trains seems odd, but the difference, I suppose, is cost. If you're paying premium prices like we are on the Ghan, you expect a higher standard of service than an everyday commuter train.

The Ghan terminal in Darwin, like the one in Adelaide, is a little way out of town, but here, there are coaches lined up ready to take us passengers to our respective hotels. Just as our coach is ready to depart, the train manager comes rushing up, shouting for BB Lookalike, who leaps up and goes to greet him. Somehow, we managed to leave not one, but both of BB Lookalike's cases behind.

After being reunited with the luggage, we settle down on the coach and make our way to our hotel. This is our second visit to Darwin, but I scarcely recognise the place thanks to a new outdoor dining and restaurant precinct close to where we are staying. Our hotel has one huge outdoor pool and a smaller indoor one.

For our first evening, we find a nondescript pizza restaurant for drinks and dinner before relishing the generous space of our room after our two nights on the train. The next day, we opt for a Red Bus city tour as we want to see indigenous art and the gallery is too far to walk. However, it is one of the stops on the bus tour.

My impression of the city is that, despite its relatively small population of around 150,000 people, it's spread out. A car would be essential if you lived here and it would need to be an air-conditioned one at that. We're lucky as it's a mild and pleasantly cool (if there is such a thing in the tropics) mid-winter day. Of course, the humidity is high, but you'd expect that this far north.

Darwin feels much more like a city in Southeast Asia than mainland Australia. The nearest major settlement in Australia, Alice Springs, is 1,500km away, a 15-and-a-half hour drive, or 2 hours and 10 minutes by air. It is half the distance to Bali in Indonesia than it is to the nation's capital, Canberra.

As we travel along on the bus, the running commentary explains why there are only a handful of houses older than 80 years along the foreshore. Darwin has been decimated by cyclones and was one of several Australian towns and cities that were bombed by the Japanese in WW2. On 19 February 1942, Japanese fighters and bombers attacked the port and ships in the harbour twice in the same day, killing over 200 Allied service personnel and civilians.

And to add to Darwin's woes, on Christmas Day 1974, the city was flattened once again, this time by tropical Cyclone Tracy, which killed 66 people and made many thousands homeless. The city that was rebuilt has a few notable buildings, including Parliament House, a white post-modern structure on the square in the centre of town.

While we are in Darwin, we run into two of the couples we dined with on the Ghan, one at the art gallery and the other down near our hotel. This brings it home to us what a small place it really is. And on the subject of dining, on our second night, we eat a casual meal at a fish restaurant close to our hotel.

The next morning, I manage a swim in the hotel pool, before packing and getting ready for the next leg of our journey, our flight to Singapore. At Darwin International Airport at check-in, my luggage allowance is 17kg over and I am stung for AU$1,017. The payment machine won't allow me to tap my phone and requires an old-fashioned chip and pin. For a while, it's touch and go. BB Lookalike and I go through three credit and debit cards before one of us finally remembers our pin number. Still, despite the excess luggage charge, we are relieved the flight is only four hours.

As we take off, I crane my neck to look out the window, watching as the Australian mainland gradually fades from view. I'll never forget this opportunity we were given, but it's now time to say goodbye. I have no regrets at leaving, as I'm sure that we'll make as good a go of being back on the other side of the world as we did in Oz.

On arrival in Singapore, we grab a cab at Changi airport and are at our hotel in half an hour. We have been upgraded to a suite and part of the package is free drinks and snacks in the business lounge. It's 7.45pm by the time we get there, and as the lounge closes at 8pm, our host comes around and offers to top our glasses up. As a result of the generous snacks on offer, we don't bother with dinner.

The next day, we have a walk along Changi Beach as

the sun is rising, before returning to our hotel for breakfast. We mistime it as there's a large tour group holidaying from China to contend with. Not only is the breakfast area packed, but it's also very hard to hang on to our table. We team tag, one guarding the seats, while the other grabs as much as we can manage from the buffet before it all goes.

We take the shuttle bus from the hotel to the airport after breakfast as our flight is at 12.35pm. We have splashed out on Premium Economy for this 14-hour flight, so we get to board early, but the seats don't seem to be all that generous compared with the premium seats on other airlines. There are, however, good headphones and restaurant-quality meals that we have been able to pre-order.

Our flight time is, in fact, 14 hours and 55 minutes as the plane has to detour around all the war zones. That's a long time to be sitting down, and despite the endless films and TV shows on offer, I can't wait to land. But landing is delayed as we hit peak evening rush hour over Heathrow. We circle around southern England in a holding pattern. I scarcely recognise it as thanks to a hot, dry summer, the fields are burnished gold rather than green.

After another ten minutes, we are given permission to land. We are met by our regular Winchester taxi driver and are very happy to greet the person who has been driving not only us, but members of our family to and from Heathrow for years. We arrive back home at 9.30pm and it's still light as it's high summer in the Northern Hemisphere.

I pinch myself as I cross the threshold. Home at last, and this time, we're staying put for the foreseeable future. Of course, there will be trips away in my capacity as the Accidental Plus One, only they'll be shorter, for weeks and months, rather than years. But for now, I relish the green, green grass of home.

. . .

Postscript

On New Year's Eve 2019, I set off with a sense of complacency, never questioning how easy it had become to move across the globe. In our interconnected world, I'd taken for granted the network of airlines bringing continents closer together. I assumed that I could hop between the UK and Australia whenever I pleased.

When that freedom was suddenly stripped away—not just from me, but from everyone—I became acutely aware of how much had changed in my lifetime. Air travel, once an unimaginable luxury, had become ordinary: as familiar to students, backpackers, families and business professionals as catching a train.

Living through the Covid-19 lockdowns in Australia, on the other side of the world from many of my family and friends, taught me never again to take people, freedoms, or opportunities for granted. And never to postpone the things that bring joy—life is shorter and more fragile than we think.

Returning to Australia in 2020 truly felt to me like third time lucky. Yet I learned that thriving in a new country doesn't just happen—you must put effort into it. Success depends so much on the attitude you bring. The more positive and open-minded you are, the more likely you'll thrive. And perhaps the most important lesson of all: don't measure the new life against the one you left behind.

I'll miss the magnificent scenery of the Outback, the light, the positive outlook that many Australians have and the friends I made. Since I've returned to my home in England, I'm learning how to be an ex-expatriate.

I'm a work in progress.

Acknowledgments

I am so grateful to Alison Jack for her meticulous and generous developmental and copy editing.

Thanks once again to Andrew Brown of Design for Writers for his imaginative book cover, which perfectly captures the tone of this memoir.

Thanks are also due to my pals in the Facebook Group We Love Memoirs, for their comments and suggestions on the manuscript.

And most of all, my heartfelt thanks go to Not Bryan Brown for all his hard graft at the day job, without which I'd never be able to write full-time.

Author Note and About the Author

Author Note

Thanks so much for reading this book. If you enjoyed it, I would love it if you would leave a review on your favourite book review website. It doesn't have to be a long one. Even a line or two makes all the difference.

About the Author

Alison Ripley Cubitt started her writing career at age nine by winning first prize in a writing competition with a pony book. Some years later, she left New Zealand with the ability to make a white sauce without a recipe, carry three plates at once, and ride a horse (though not at the same time). Dreaming of becoming a copywriter, she landed a job as the receptionist in an advertising agency in Sydney that made the TV series Mad Men's work culture look tame.

But the lure of London proved too hard to resist, and she left Australia. Landing in London at the right time, she got her break in television production and lasted 15 years, working on Channel 4's anarchic The Big Breakfast and at Walt Disney and the BBC.

For the past five and a half years, she has divided her time between Melbourne, Australia and Jane Austen country, England.

An accomplished author of non-fiction works,

including two travel guides and four memoirs, her literary achievements encompass works of fiction, from screenplays to short stories and thrillers. *The Accidental Plus One Down Under: Travel Tales from a Trailing Spouse* is her tenth published book.

Also by Alison Ripley Cubitt

Memoirs: The Accidental Plus One: Travel Tales from a
Trailing Spouse

https://mybook.to/TAPO

Castles in the Air

https://mybook.to/CastlesintheAir

Misadventures in the Screen Trade

https://mybook.to/MsAdventures

Fiction: Revolution Earth by Lambert Nagle

https://mybook.to/StephenConnor1

Nighthawks by Lambert Nagle

https://mybook.to/StephenConnor2

Non Fiction: Finding a Home in Aotearoa New Zealand

https://mybook.to/FindaHomeNZ

If you love reading and writing memoirs, join us!

www.facebook.com/groups/welovememoirs

Printed in Dunstable, United Kingdom